Jackie

Mel Mullen

EXPERIENCE
JESUS AND HIS CHURCH

*Enjoy the
31 Day
Journey
Mel Mullen*

A Journey to a Greater Spiritual Life.

Published 2018
Jaquith Creative, Bothell, Washington, USA

Printed in Canada

ISBN-13: 978-0-9849082-6-4
22 21 20 19 18   1 2 3 4 5
Library of Congress Control Number: 2018958299

Cover design and book layout by Ignacio Huizar. www.nachohuizar.com

Also available in e-book and audio book formats. For more information or to order in bulk, contact info@jaquithcreative.com.

Praise for Experience Jesus and His Church

BRIAN HOUSTON, GLOBAL SENIOR PASTOR, HILLSONG CHURCH, AUSTRALIA:
Mel Mullen is a seasoned follower of Jesus Christ and builder of His Church. With reassuring scholarliness and the valuable wisdom of years, he skillfully unwraps the mystery of the relationship between Christ and His Church—its foundations, values, beliefs, culture, and leadership. He also offers insight and clarity to often overlooked or misunderstood teachings while weaving personal stories and experiences along the way. We owe a great deal to the generations upon whose shoulders we continue to build the Church, and I believe much gold is found written on the hearts of faithful people such as Mel Mullen.

TOMMY BARNETT, CO-PASTOR, DREAM CITY CHURCH, PHOENIX; FOUNDER AND CO-PASTOR, THE DREAM CENTER, LOS ANGELES:
This book is filled with real stories and truths that will reshape your understanding about who Jesus is and what a local church can be. *Experience Jesus and His Church* is a must-read for leaders who want to build a successful, relevant, and people-reaching church.

KEVIN GERALD, LEAD PASTOR, CHAMPIONS CENTRE, TACOMA, WASHINGTON:
My friend Pastor Mel Mullen has been a great leader and church builder for many years. His passion, experience, and ability to articulate the vision provide tremendous insight for church leadership and teams.

MATTHEW BARNETT, CO-FOUNDER, THE DREAM CENTER, AND SENIOR PASTOR, ANGELUS TEMPLE, LOS ANGELES, CALIFORNIA:

Pastor Mel's leadership has meant so much to me in my life. Mel has the unique ability to connect with new believers and individuals who are mature in their faith. *Experience Jesus and His Church* does exactly that. This book offers so much wisdom to the body of Christ, and no matter what season of life you are in, it will greatly benefit you.

DINO RIZZO, EXECUTIVE DIRECTOR, ASSOCIATION OF RELATED CHURCHES (ARC):

I always love it when someone truly champions the local church. I believe with all my heart that it is the hope this world needs—not just great church services but the bride of Christ—people who believe and know Jesus as their Savior and their hope, spreading that hope to a broken community. In this book I've found another champion—Mel Mullen—and I am thankful for his voice coming from such a deep well of experience. This is most definitely a book I hope every pastor will read and learn from.

DONNA CROUCH, COMMUNITY ENGAGEMENT PASTOR, HILLSONG CHURCH:

I first met Mel and Heather at our Hillsong Conference many years ago in Sydney, Australia. Then, a handful of years ago, the opportunity for me to visit Home Church came my way. It was breathtaking! When God moves on a group of people, I don't believe you can reduce it to a formula. A move of God is just that—it is sovereign, divine, and beyond our ability to manufacture. However, there are principles and values that He blesses and breathes on which we need to understand and pass on to this new generation. I believe this book will help you capture the heart, the why behind the what, the battles and lessons that have been won, and the values and passion that are now seeing the influence of Home Church reach nations. I know it will help you as you endeavor to play your part in what Jesus is doing in His Church for such a time as this!

DEBBIE BOLTON, CO-FOUNDER AND GLOBAL CHIEF SALES OFFICER, NORWEX:
I have known Pastor Mel for almost twenty years and I continue to see his passion to build the church and equip people. He lives daily the truths talked about in this book, and I am honored to know him and recommend this book to anyone who also wants to live purposefully and be part of building the church.

STEVE MURRELL, PRESIDENT, EVERY NATION CHURCHES & MINISTRIES, AND FOUNDING PASTOR, VICTORY MANILA, MANILA, PHILIPPINES:
If you want to live a life of faithfulness and leave a legacy of faith, this book is for you. For more than three decades, Mel has been a faithful friend, one who has never failed to stretch my faith and refresh my soul. Years ago, Mel went to Red Deer on a thirty-day mission trip that never ended. He felt God's call to a community that needed the gospel, and he faithfully followed. Mel's leadership has resulted in a church that is impacting individuals, communities, cities, and nations all over the world. I hope this book inspires you to live a life of global and multi-generational impact.

REV. RICHARD CIARAMITARO, PRESIDENT, OPEN BIBLE FAITH FELLOWSHIP OF CANADA:
Pastor Mel has truly modeled, built, and invested his life in passion for the local church and its mission to expand and break out by impacting the hearts and lives of people through the gospel. The stories of transformed lives and teachings in *Experience Jesus and His Church* are practical and applicable for new and older believers alike. I believe reading and practicing these truths will create a solid foundation for believers to walk out their journey of faith and encourage them to connect and serve in a local church.

AKI MIZUNO, FOUNDER, FAMILY OF GOD CHURCHES, JAPAN:
This is a very helpful and practical book. I can recommend it to everyone and anyone. I've known Mel and Heather for many

years, and their experiences with people, whether at church or in the marketplace, are real and good examples. Their desire to see many people welcomed into a personal faith with Jesus Christ never ceases to amaze me—not only a personal experience, which we all need, but a community one as well: to feel welcome and "at home" with God's family. This book will help Christians and Christian leaders grow and be more mature. I especially appreciate that Mel emphasizes that everything should be Jesus-centered.

DR. DAVID CANNISTRACI, LEAD PASTOR, GATEWAY CITY CHURCH, SAN JOSE, CALIFORNIA:

In *Experience Jesus and His Church*, my lifelong friend Pastor Mel Mullen has captured the heart and soul of how each of us can live out our God-given purpose. This unique book is important because we all need a clear starting point for our calling in life. That starting point is the local church—about which Jesus stated, "I will build my Community and the gates of She'ol will not overcome it" (Matthew 16:18, CJB). You were created to "experience Jesus and His Church." If you are committed to living for Him and experiencing all that He has for your future, get this book and read it. You will be on your way to the greatest experience of your life!

MICAH PELKEY, LEAD PASTOR, STORYSIDE CHURCH, BELLVILLE, OHIO:

There is so much noise in our lives that sometimes knowing what is important and what is not is difficult to distinguish. Mel Mullen does a magnificent job of cutting through all the noise and confusion and reinforcing that two things stand firm: Jesus and His Church. He shows us how both are as relevant today as they were nearly two thousand years ago.

KEN MILES, PRESIDENT, ANCHOR MINISTERIAL FELLOWSHIP:

Mel Mullen's most recent book, *Experience Jesus and His Church*, is well-named. In it, the author has distilled five decades of ministry and pastoral experience into one book. What a masterpiece! It is a biographical history, study guide, devotional, and practical "how to" book all woven into one. The insights on Christ and His Church are relevant to both new Christians as well as seasoned pastors. Be sure to read this book and gain wisdom and knowledge from this successful pastor and church.

REV. M.D. (MEL) DAVIS, PRESIDENT, INTERNATIONAL ASSOCIATION OF MINISTRIES, CANADA:

Mel Mullen's book *Experience Jesus and His Church* is a scriptural pattern and process for believers and churches to follow. Every pastor, leader, and member should have this book. It shows the way for success and contentment today. What a privilege to experience building with our Lord! We must fulfill the divine call. This book is an excellent teaching tool for churches and individuals. It is not only good, but satisfying.

DR. PHIL NORDIN, CHAIRMAN, EQUIP INTERNATIONAL:

Pastor Mel Mullen has taken on the daunting task of articulating timeless principles with a fresh approach. The testimonies and stories in his latest book, *Experience Jesus and His Church*, add color and sparkle to the truths we all know well. Mel has always trumpeted the message of building strong local churches, and his love for this divine institution shines in every chapter. In this writing, Mel has made the Church "cool" again. It is a must-read for every leader and certainly every believer.

JOHN P. KELLY, JOHN P. KELLY MINISTRIES AND INTERNATIONAL COALITION OF APOSTOLIC LEADERS:

Experience Jesus and His Church, by Mel Mullen, gives us the two most important themes of the Old and New Testament: Jesus as the Messiah and the Church as the Congregation of God. Mullen uses expert biblical exegesis as a complete proof text of Jesus and His Church. He shares profound wisdom that comes from the knowledge of God's word and the leading of His Holy Spirit, plus his many personal experiences as a church planter, builder, and leader. In this book, which is sprinkled with testimonies of those who have experienced Jesus and the fulfillment of His church, Mullen makes the case for Christ and His Church. Presented by a true apostolic leader, this is more than a scholarly read; it is truly a must-read experience!

DR. CANUTE B. BLAKE, LEAD PASTOR, NEW LIFE COVENANT CENTRE (CHURCH OF GOD) AND FOUNDER AND PRESIDENT, NEW LIFE GLOBAL HARVEST MINISTRIES INC.:

Mel Mullen's purpose for writing this book is to challenge and encourage readers to experience Jesus Christ at work in their lives through the Church. He reminds us that it was Jesus who created the Church as a place where we can encounter and experience an authentic relationship with God. This book is a must-read for every Christian who wants to serve the Lord effectively by being a productive member of the Body of Christ (the Church). Mel Mullen is truly a passionate follower of Christ who loves the local church and has seen the mighty hand of God at work in communities large and small, in cities, in nations, and in the global sphere.

ALBERTO CARBONE, SENIOR PASTOR, MCI, MONTREAL, CANADA:

God has inspired my brother Mullen, an apostolic leader with years of experience, to write this valuable book to be an inheritance for the generation to come and to equip churches for their calling. His experiences are precious keys for Christians to receive a fresh and enlightened perspective about fundamental knowledge for building a healthy and conquering church. I enjoyed going through the well-explained beliefs, values, cultures, and leadership lessons. You will be blessed by this gift of God.

DR. JAMES MAROCCO, SENIOR PASTOR, KING'S CATHEDRAL, HAWAII:
I've known Mel Mullen for a number of years. Jesus said, "I will build my church and the gates of hell shall not prevail against it." Mel Mullen has written a book that will help a pastor or a parishioner get a fresh look at the church. The testimonies, the insights, and the ways God has worked in and through Mel and Home Church will inspire you to be a part of joining Jesus in building His church, not only in your community, but worldwide.

TABLE OF CONTENTS (CONTINUED)

SECTION 4: CULTURE · *What you see and what you feel*

SECTION 5: LEAD THE WAY · *The church that changes the world*

Let's Become Friends

Mel Mullen and his wife, Heather, founded what is now Home Church (originally the People's Church and later Word of Life Church) in 1972. Home Church is an ever-growing, multi-site church with over one hundred locations around the world and many more on the horizon. In recent years, they transitioned the lead pastorate of the church to their son and daughter-in-law, Jachin and Becca Mullen. Their daughter Christy and her husband Chad are also essential leaders on the team.

Mel and Heather are very active in ministry. At home, they continue to serve the vision of Home Church Canada under the direction of Lead Pastors Jachin and Becca and the leadership team. They also travel extensively, giving oversight to Home Church locations in many nations. They speak regularly at conferences, leadership events, and churches in the larger body of Christ.

Their vision is to fulfill the Great Commission, make disciples of Jesus, train leaders, and build God's great church in the world. They believe that the gospel of Jesus is the good news of salvation and that the church Jesus is building today is the greatest entity on earth. They know that in God's great plan, every local church should grow and impact the community, and they are committed to inspiring and equipping local churches to do just that.

Besides their two children, Jachin and Christy, Mel and Heather have six amazing grandchildren. They are thrilled to all be working together as a family in ministry, and they are excited to see what God has in store for every generation to come.

Foreword

BY JOE CHAMPION

The church, you see, is not peripheral to the world; the world is peripheral to the church. The church is Christ's body, in which he speaks and acts, by which he fills everything with his presence.
(Ephesians 1:23 MSG)

The Church. The Bride. The Body of Christ. The Family of God. Christ died for her, established her, protects her, and is coming back for her. For all that humankind has tried to do to destroy her, and for all of the human flaws within her, there is nothing Jesus loves more than His church.

I wasn't raised in church. My Sundays were spent on the sidelines as a ball boy, watching my father coach in the Canadian and National Football Leagues. When he retired and we moved to Mississippi, our neighbors came over and promised to take me to the Carriage House restaurant for their famous fried chicken, but only if I went to church with them first. I went for the chicken, but I got the church! Little did I know how much that day would forever change my life. I fell in love with Jesus, but I also fell in love with His church. And what an impact the church has continued to make in my life over the last almost forty years, from being set free from sin, to meeting my wife, to finding my calling, to seeing my children meet Jesus and find their callings, to having served in the ministry for almost thirty years and pastoring a thriving church!

I love the church. As Christ-followers, we should all love the church. You can't love Jesus without loving His bride. That is why I'm so excited about this book: about the stories of lives changed and the truth of God's vision and heart for the church within its pages. It will make you fall in love all over again. It will make you step up your commitment to what Christ was and continues to be so committed to!

More than twenty-two years ago, I was a young pastor at a small church in the swamps of south Louisiana, looking for fellowship and mentorship. During that season, my wife and I met Pastors Mel and Heather Mullen. Little did we know that we were making friends for life.

I remember our first visit to the church they founded in Red Deer, Alberta. When we saw all they were doing, and when we experienced their services and their staff and volunteers, it took our breath away and stretched us to do more! We've visited every year since then, and I'm always inspired by Pastor Mel's continued passion and energy to advance and build the church, locally and globally.

This book is lived out over many decades, but the message is timeless and has never been more timely. The writer of Hebrews gives this challenge to us, especially as the world becomes increasingly darker and more chaotic. *"Let us hold fast the confession of our hope without wavering, for He who promised is faithful; and let us consider how to stimulate one another to love and good deeds, not forsaking our own assembling together, as is the habit of some, but encouraging one another; and all the more, as you see the day drawing near."* (Hebrews 10:23-25 NASB)

THE ANSWER TO EVERY ISSUE WE ARE FACING IN TODAY'S WORLD IS TO EXPERIENCE JESUS AND HIS CHURCH!

I almost died on an airplane recently.

If that sounds dramatic, it's because it was dramatic. It was also a bit embarrassing. I wasn't in a plane wreck or anything of the sort. I simply had some heart trouble at one of the most inconvenient moments imaginable: while flying in a hollow tube across the sky. Later, I would find out that a section of my heart had stopped working properly; but during that flight, all I knew was something was very wrong.

There wasn't a lot they could do in the air. They took my pulse, gave me three bottles of oxygen, and offered me orange juice. I had to be rushed to the hospital as soon as we landed. If it would have been a longer flight, I wouldn't have made it.

Two days and two pacemakers later, I was basically back to my normal self. I've never been one to lie around for long. My doctors made me cancel all international travel for a couple of months, but that just gave me more time to work on this book, so I can't complain. And my heart and I have been together for a long time—over seventy years—so it can be forgiven for a hiccup or two.

All that to say, I've had a lot of time to think recently. There's nothing like a medical emergency at thirty thousand feet to make you evaluate your life.

The word that most describes what I feel is gratitude. I'm grateful for life and health. I'm grateful for my kids, my family, my friends, and my church. I'm beyond grateful for my wife, who has put up with me for forty-eight years and counting. I'm certainly grateful for doctors and medical technology. But most of all, I'm grateful for Jesus. I am a happy, fulfilled man, and the grace and love of Jesus have carried me to where I am.

I'm also filled with gratitude that for nearly half a century now, I've had the privilege of working with and for local churches. It's been a wonderful run so far—and I'm not even close to being finished yet. I believe the best is still to come.

During those years, I've seen both the good side and the difficult side of church life. Nobody is perfect, as I'm sure you are aware; and since churches are made up of imperfect people, no church is perfect, either. But church is still a wonderful, incomparable, life-transforming gift from God. There is nothing I would rather do with my life than help people experience Jesus, and the church is the best vehicle I've found to do just that.

The purpose of this book is to help you experience Jesus at work in your life, and in particular to experience Him through the vehicle of the local church. The church has many times been misunderstood, criticized, or rejected; but over the course of my life, I've seen how important and effective it is in helping us follow Jesus. The goal of life is not church: the goal is Jesus. But it was Jesus who created the church as the ideal environment to meet with Him, know Him, serve Him, and help others know Him.

Throughout this book, I have included the personal stories of many friends who have experienced Jesus and His church in specific ways. Their stories not only illustrate the principles and truths communicated in these pages, but they are a testimony to the love, grace, and power of God to change lives.

Although the Bible deals with hundreds—maybe even thousands—of topics and questions, there are two overarching themes that run throughout it. These themes are present in both the Old and New Testaments, and they tie together the entire narrative of Scripture. These two themes are *Jesus* and *His church*.

I don't think most people would argue about Jesus being the central theme of Scripture. His life and His salvation were predicted from the very beginning of the Bible. Immediately after the fall of man and the entrance of sin in the world, God promised to send a savior, a rescuer. In Genesis 3:15, He told the snake, the devil, that a descendent of Adam and Eve would "bruise your head, and you shall bruise his heel." It was a poetic metaphor referring to Jesus' ultimate victory over sin and Satan on the cross.

The entire Old Testament is full of references to Jesus' redemption of humanity. Israel was commanded to offer sacrifices for sin, which symbolized Jesus' sacrifice on the cross. Prophet after prophet predicted in great detail what Jesus' life and death would look like, including His place of birth, His childhood in Nazareth, His ministry to the poor and broken, His brutal crucifixion, His resurrection, and His eternal rule as Lord of the universe.

The Gospels record Jesus' birth, ministry, and redemptive work. The rest of the New Testament is the story of Jesus' ongoing involvement in humanity through the church. It ends with Revelation, a prophetic message from Jesus that encourages us to remain true until the end because we will see Him again.

The Bible is not only about Jesus—it's also about His church. They always go together. The book of Ephesians goes so far as to call the church the bride of Christ and to say that Jesus and the church are one body that is inextricably joined (Ephesians 5:22-32).

The church is made up of all those who follow Jesus. It is visible even in the Old Testament: the nation of Israel was called the "congregation in the wilderness" (Acts 7:38 ESV). Moses led this great "church" through the wilderness to the Promised Land. Centuries later, David made plans for the temple, which his son Solomon built. Throughout the story of Israel, God was present among His people, and His people were the church.

When Jesus took His disciples to Caesarea Philippi, He said, "I will build my church" (Matthew 16:18). The book of Acts describes how the Holy Spirit worked through Christians to establish churches throughout the Roman empire. The Epistles (letters) that make up much of the New Testament were written to the churches in Rome, Ephesus, Galatia, Thessalonica, Colossae, Philippi, and other regions. The letters to Timothy and Titus contained instructions to young leaders about how to lead and build great churches. The New Testament concludes with Revelation, a book written by John to the seven churches of Asia Minor.

Since the church is so important to Jesus, and since it figures so prominently in Scripture, it should be important to you and me as well. How can we receive the greatest benefit possible from this life-giving gift? How can we help others benefit from it? How can we play our part in building the church?

In the following pages, I am going to answer those questions. I will present a variety of truths and topics that are essential to a life-giving experience in church. Whether you are a church leader, a pastor, a member of a church, a new believer, or someone who is still making up your mind what you believe about Jesus, this book is for you!

I hope with all my heart (and both my pacemakers) that this book opens your mind and heart to all God has in store for you through His church. Let's believe together that for all of us, our best is yet to come!

Sincerely,

PASTOR *Mel Mullen*

LET'S GET STARTED
The basics of the Christian life

Never the Same
An experience with Jesus changes everything.

IN THE EARLY 1970s, throughout North America, young people had bought into the doctrine of Woodstock. In the name of love and peace, they were caught up in drugs, alcohol, and free love. They were fueled in part by famous singers and other public voices. The result on university campuses across the continent was a flood of addiction, excess, and emptiness that would eventually become synonymous with that decade.

In the middle of the emptiness, however, the Holy Spirit began moving across the continent in a powerful way. Young people found Christ, left behind their old ways of life, and placed their futures in God's hands.

These young people had the same fervor but a new message. *Repent! Jesus Loves You! Turn or Burn!* Their slogans were carried on signs in Jesus marches across North America's cities as thousands of young people paraded their new freedom and faith in Christ.

The small city of Red Deer, Alberta, Canada, was no exception. Young people who had been addicted to drugs and alcohol found deliverance by accepting Jesus Christ. They left the highs offered by the drug culture and began to experience a new reality, a new hope—one that could only be found in knowing Jesus.

It was into this raw and thrilling new environment of young people finding Jesus that my wife, Heather, and I arrived. Little did we know that our story and Red Deer's story would become forever intertwined.

Prior to our arrival, we had been youth pastors in a traditional church in Vancouver for some time. We became intrigued by what God was doing in the Jesus People and Charismatic movements along the west coast of Canada. We had a great desire to help youth find Christ, and we longed to experience the renewal that was taking place in many churches.

We visited communes where some of the Jesus people lived. We attended charismatic and interfaith services where hundreds of people were being filled with the Holy Spirit. Soon, we found personal renewal and experienced a new baptism with the Holy Spirit.

Over time, we sensed God leading us to transition out of our church and into a ministry that we knew He would show us. After completing our work in Vancouver, we began to speak in churches across Canada. Along the way, we visited Red Deer for what was supposed to be a thirty-day mission. God had other plans, though.

A SIMPLE MESSAGE

At the time, Red Deer was a rather religious-minded town of just twenty-seven thousand people. Numerous young people had come to Christ, but being the radical and non-traditional kind of individuals they were, no churches in Red Deer were ready to receive them. At the time, carrying big Bibles and speaking in tongues was not acceptable to most of the churches of the city.

We came with a simple message: *Jesus loves you and has a wonderful plan for your life.* Young people flocked to a message of love, acceptance, and freedom in Jesus. Within weeks of our arrival in Red Deer, the news media carried the story of changed lives.

Our thirty-day mission ended, but we couldn't leave. As we saw Jesus' freedom and grace so tangibly manifested around us, something happened in our hearts. We knew God was calling us to this place. We were captivated by a God-given vision of a church community that would embrace and disciple these passionate young people. We decided to settle in Red Deer and begin a new church with this youth movement. Within a short few years, thousands of Alberta's young people experienced salvation, were baptized in water, and were filled with the Holy Spirit.

As our church grew from one season to another, it went through many changes in keeping with the times. What began as a small group of misfit youth has now grown into a multisite, international church that is reaching thousands of people every week. The good news has gone out from our church to the continents of the world, and amazing church branches have been formed in many nations. Truly there is no limit to what God can accomplish!

IS IT POSSIBLE TODAY?

The stories of thousands of changed lives brings me to these questions: Is the message of the good news of salvation relevant for us today? Is it really possible for people to have a personal encounter with Jesus Christ and, in a moment, have their lives saved and their futures turned around? Is it possible for sins to be forgiven and a new life established? Is it possible to be freed from addictions and live a pure and clean life? Is it possible to be healed and made totally whole? Is it possible to have a second chance at life, to be complete in body, soul, and spirit? Is it possible to experience abundant life on earth and eternal life in heaven through knowing Jesus?

The answer is a resounding, absolute *yes*! I am glad to report that the good news of Jesus was not just a message for a short time or for a small city in Canada. It is a message that has brought deliverance, healing, and wholeness to thousands of people. The experience those young people had is the same experience people are having today. There is deliverance from drug addiction. There is healing from sickness and disease. There is mental wellness. All of this and more are part of the fullness of life people can experience when they follow Jesus Christ. This experience can happen in an instant when they decide to make Jesus the Lord of their lives. God's desire for every life is immediate, total salvation followed by a lifestyle of healing, deliverance, and wholeness.

THREE LIFE-CHANGING EXPERIENCES

This experience of radical conversion is first found in Acts 2. In one day, three thousand people repented of their sins, were baptized, and received the Holy Spirit. These three experiences became the foundation of the first Christian church, and they continue to be relevant today.

The first experience is *repentance*, when a person turns to Jesus and is brought into salvation. The second experience is *water baptism*, which symbolizes our pasts being buried with Jesus in his death and our lives being made new through his resurrection. The third experience is the *baptism with the Holy Spirit*, which provides the empowerment to live the Christian life.

The word *salvation* in Greek, which was the original language of the New Testament, simply means to be delivered, protected, rescued, or brought to wholeness or safety. It has the idea of being healed physically, morally, and spiritually.

This is exactly what Jesus did for people in the Bible when they came to Him and asked for His help. This was the message Jesus communicated when He asked people, "Would you like to be made well?" And this is what He continues to do today. He delivers us from sin, He brings our minds, emotions, and wills to wholeness, and often He even heals our bodies. Salvation is an immediate experience that is followed by a process of bringing us to fullness and abundance of life.

Jesus does this for anyone who comes to Him. Whether you have known Him your whole life or are just now beginning to believe in Him, Jesus accepts you and loves you unconditionally. You can experience salvation and fullness of life through His love.

THINGS TO THINK ABOUT

1. How is the message of salvation relevant to you today?

2. Describe your personal encounter with Jesus.

3. How has your life been changed through your experience with Jesus?

Brad's Story

THIS IS MY *story about how God completely changed my world. I was born into a Christian family. It was just my mom and me at the beginning. She is an amazing woman of God who did everything for me. Then she met my dad. My dad and I instantly clicked. We had found the man who would stand with us for the rest of our lives.*

As a young teen I gave my heart to Jesus, but I never really gave Him my life. I was about twelve years old the first time I went drinking. Around the same age, I looked at pornography for the first time. I still went to church with my parents, but it was a weekly chore for me. A few years passed, and I tried drugs for the first time. By the time I was fifteen, I was getting into drugs and alcohol a couple times a week.

Around that time my dad was transferred for work, and we had to move away. That was a really difficult transition for me. I went from having everyone to having no one. But after we moved, we reconnected with some old friends we hadn't seen since I was very young. Their kids were going to the same high school I was going to. These friends were the first good influences I had in my life.

I started going to church every week. I even joined the youth group where I met some of my best friends to this day. I had a love for Jesus and I wanted to serve Him, but I still wasn't ready to give Him everything.

I spent a couple of years in the church, but most of my friends gradually left. Eventually I left, too, because I felt like there was nothing at the church for me anymore. I made many friends at school who invited me to parties, and I soon found myself completely ensnared in everything I had once walked away from.

When I do something, I do it all or nothing. So I partied, and I partied hard. I skipped almost a full semester of Grade 12 just to meet my friends at the bar. I lived like this for about four years. I was completely separated from the church, and I was no longer serving the Lord whatsoever. I found myself partying harder and becoming an angrier and more self-conscious person.

I didn't think I deserved much love, so I settled for any love that anybody was willing to give me. I began sleeping around. I always felt filthy afterward, but the more I drank, the more it didn't matter. I had a couple of girlfriends who said they loved me, but they only showed it when they were getting something out of me. I gave my money, love, body, and ambition to these girls and in return received a very shallow "love."

I fell into a dark place after my girlfriend at the time said she just wanted to be friends but still wanted to sleep with me. Sex without love is nothing at all. I began to have anxiety attacks and suicidal thoughts. I had never felt further from God. My drug use became very heavy. I was spending most of my money on a high or a night out.

I hit rock bottom. I cried out to God and asked if there was any way I could see Him again. I prayed like that for months without really knowing why I was praying it. All I knew was I couldn't live like this anymore. Little did I know, during that time my parents were on their knees every day praying for me.

Then one night something happened that changed my heart completely. God met me in my bedroom. It was just Him and me, and it was the most real experience I have ever had in my life. He changed my thinking. He changed my heart. I started going to the church my parents attended, and I found a home. I found God's grace.

I decided to give God my absolute everything. I gave Him my addictions, my hurt, my sin, my future, and my life. After this decision, I couldn't have even guessed where He would take me. I have never been so close to God, and I honestly have never been happier. God even gave me someone who showed me what it really means to be in love.

My only response to what God has done for me is to praise Him, to live for His glory, and to give to His house. God flipped my world upside down! I don't deserve this, and I thank Jesus for it. I will live for Him because His love for me has always been there and will always be there. He had me in His hands from day one. He has a plan for my life, and I can't even imagine where He'll take me from here.

Following Jesus
Disciples are made, not just born.

IN THOSE EARLY years in Red Deer, young people by the hundreds came to know Jesus. Previously, they had been caught up in lifestyles of drugs, addiction, and rebellion. Then they met God, and they found a new life of freedom. They found peace as they put their faith in Jesus and learned a new way of living. It was an incredible, exhilarating experience to watch them discover the life only God gives.

This should happen for everyone who meets Jesus. When you believe in Him and come to know and love Him, your life begins to change. It's a natural, wonderful process the Bible calls discipleship. Simply put, being a disciple means following Jesus. It means turning your life over to Him in faith and humility.

The people flocking to our church wanted to know God better. They needed to find practical, tangible freedom from old ways of living. We began to teach them principles of faith, obedience, authority, and healthy relationships. In those early days in Red Deer, we quickly discovered that true disciples are *made*, not just *born*.

IT'S A PROCESS

After Jesus was resurrected, in the moments before He ascended into heaven, He gave His disciples a parting command.

Remember, these men had been with Jesus for three and a half years. They had seen His love for the lost, His compassion for people, and His faith in God. They had spent countless hours listening as He told them what it meant to live a life of faith and obedience on a practical, day-to-day level.

> Therefore, go and make disciples of all the nations, baptizing them in the name of the Father and the Son and the Holy Spirit. Teach these new disciples to obey all the commands I have given you. And be sure of this: I am with you always, even to the end of the age.
> (Matthew 28:19-20)

This parting command is known as the Great Commission. The Great Commission was an all-inclusive command to make disciples, baptize, and teach. It is clear in Jesus' words that there is a *process* to discipleship. When people come to Christ, they need to be baptized and taught. They need to take steps in following Jesus. Believing in Jesus leads to following Jesus, and following Jesus means growing, changing, obeying, and becoming more like Him. It means learning to look like Jesus and live like Jesus.

FOLLOW ME

One day, when Jesus was walking by the sea of Galilee, He was introduced to Peter, Philip, and Nathanael. These young men instantly believed Jesus was the Messiah.

Days later, Jesus was walking along the seashore and encountered Peter, James, and John with their fishing boat and gear. They had fished all night and caught nothing. He told them to let their nets down into the water again. In obedience to Christ, they let down the nets—and ended up filling two boats with the fish they caught. Jesus said, "Follow me," and they left their nets and became His disciples.

That was just the beginning. Jesus invited businessmen, tax collectors, rebels, and people from many other walks of life to leave all and follow Him. His twelve disciples were an unexpected mix of professionals, blue-collar workers, and misfits with one thing in common: they made an immediate change in their lifestyles when Jesus said, "Follow Me."

Being a disciple doesn't mean you are perfect. Some people hesitate to commit to Jesus because they aren't sure they can live up to some standard of perfection. I have news for you—none of us can. These original twelve disciples were far from perfect. The Bible reveals their weaknesses and errors time and time again. I find that encouraging! Being a disciple is about heart, not performance. It's about commitment, not perfection. And most importantly of all, it's about relationship. A disciple is someone who is *with* Jesus, *follows* Jesus, and *listens* to Jesus.

In the early days of our church, we developed six steps in becoming a follower of Jesus Christ. Our goal was to help new believers become true disciples and experience the abundant, free, holy lifestyle Jesus desired for them.

STEP 1: ASSURANCE OF SALVATION

The *assurance* of salvation is an important part of the *experience* of salvation. You must have an inner confidence that you have been born again.

When you first believe in Jesus, it's common to experience doubts that seem to undermine your faith. You need to learn to walk by faith, not by feelings, and to establish your beliefs on the Word of God.

The apostle John wrote, "I have written this to you who believe in the name of the Son of God, so that you may know you have eternal life" (1 John 5:13). You know you are saved because the Word of God declares you are saved. When you align your faith with the Bible, you receive an unshakable assurance of salvation.

STEP 2: WATER BAPTISM

In the early days of our church, baptism often took place on the day of salvation. People responded to the call to receive Christ and immediately went into the water to be baptized. This is what took place in the early church as well. People heard the message of Jesus, were baptized, and were filled with the Holy Spirit on the same day. I urge new followers of Jesus to be baptized as soon as possible. Don't wait—follow the example of Jesus and be baptized. It is a life-changing experience in your walk with Jesus.

Baptize in the original language means "to dip." Baptism was by immersion in the New Testament and the early church, and I believe it is the best method today.

Water baptism is a public declaration of your faith in Christ, and it is a letting go of the past. The blood of Jesus totally cleansed you from sin when you were saved, and baptism is a symbolic, spiritual act of obedience that declares you have new life in Jesus (Romans 6:3-4).

STEP 3: BAPTISM WITH THE HOLY SPIRIT

At the moment of salvation, the Holy Spirit began to dwell in you. But that was just the beginning. You can also experience the infilling of the Holy Spirit (also called the baptism with the Holy Spirit) which empowers you to live the Christian life and to follow Him. Jesus stated to His disciples on His last day with them, "You will receive power after the Holy Spirit has come upon you. And you will be my witnesses . . ." (Acts 1:8). We will discuss this in greater detail in a later chapter.

The baptism with the Holy Spirit is for every follower of Jesus, and a new prayer language is available to everyone who receives the Holy Spirit. This language, also called speaking in tongues, is useful to the believer for daily prayer and communication with God (Acts 2:1-4; 1 Corinthians 14:1-18).

STEP 4: DAILY RELATIONSHIP WITH GOD

You can grow in relationship with God daily by reading His Word. The Bible reveals God's will, thoughts, and plans for your life. God speaks through His Word, and it is His guide for daily living. As you read the Bible, you will often find that verses come alive to you. They will speak to specific circumstances and needs. This is one of the most common ways God directs us and helps us.

The psalmist wrote, "I have hidden your word in my heart, that I might not sin against you" (Psalm 119:11). Later in the same psalm he says, "Your word is a lamp to guide my feet and a light for my path" (Psalm 119:105).

STEP 5: LORDSHIP OF JESUS CHRIST

Jesus is both Savior and Lord. He does not just save you from your sins and deliver you from the issues of your past—He wants to be the Lord of your life.

Discipleship is "whole life training." It means living in obedience to Christ and doing His will. You can't be a part-time disciple, and there is no such thing as partial obedience or partial submission to God. You are either fully committed to Jesus or you are not. Later in His ministry, Jesus said to some of His followers, "Why do you keep calling me 'Lord, Lord!' when you don't do what I say?" (Luke 6:46).

Being a disciple doesn't mean quitting your day job and becoming a full-time minister. It simply means that in everything you do, you strive to follow Jesus' teachings and example. Learning to live in obedience to Christ and His commands is essential to being a disciple of Jesus Christ.

STEP 6: GOD'S CHURCH

When we are born again by the Holy Spirit at the point of our salvation, God adopts us into His family. Part of being in His family is attending and participating in a local church. Often it is through attending, receiving, and giving in a local community that you discover fulfillment and purpose in life. If you want to flourish and grow in God, you need to be in His house.

Psalm 92:12-13 says, "The righteous will flourish like a palm tree, they will grow like a cedar of Lebanon; planted in the house of the Lord, they will flourish in the courts of our God" (NIV).

Jesus is extending the same invitation He gave to his disciples to you and me: "Follow Me!" He has invited all of us into His discipleship program. Every person has a different background, but we face the same question: Will we be true followers and disciples of Jesus Christ?

THINGS TO THINK ABOUT

1. If you've been baptized in water, describe the experience. What does it mean to you?

2. Have you received the baptism in the Holy Spirit with a prayer language? Are you using your prayer language every day?

3. What does your personal relationship with God look like on a daily basis?

4. What does it mean to you that Jesus should be your Lord, not just your Savior?

5. What benefits have you seen in your life from being planted in the house of God, the church?

DAY 3

I *Can* See It

Every church and every follower
of Jesus needs a God-given vision.

IT WAS A Tuesday night in March 1972. We were holding a small prayer meeting with a few of the new followers of Jesus in a basement suite in Red Deer. The place was not luxurious—"dumpy" would be a more accurate term. The toilet often would not flush, and we drank coffee from borrowed, stained dishes.

We believed God would answer prayer, and we believed He would speak to us when we asked Him for direction. I was leading the prayer group, and I remember praying, "God, what is Your plan for this group?" At the time, we were not even a church. We were simply a movement of youth in the small city of Red Deer, Alberta.

As we prayed, one of the members of the group suddenly spoke up. He said, "I believe God is showing me a picture of a big wheel with a hub that is on fire. There are spokes extending from the hub that are also on fire, and at the end of each spoke, there is another fire."

That was both exciting and perplexing. We didn't know what God was saying. We prayed some more and asked for His help to understand the vision we felt He was showing us. As we discussed the picture the Holy Spirit had given us, we came to understand we were to share the good news of Jesus to the surrounding rural communities and form groups of believers in every community.

Soon we launched outreach efforts that took the good news of Jesus to the streets of the surrounding communities in rural Alberta. As people found Christ, we formed Bible study groups in several communities. Some of these groups grew to become Sunday morning services and eventually church locations that exist to this day.

At the time, our little group didn't have a vision large enough to extend beyond Canada. However, after thirty-five years of building a "One Church" model in Canada, the Holy Spirit again spoke to us. He showed us we were to take the One Church model to the nations of the world. Now we are one church with locations all around the world.

THE VISION MUST BE CONFIRMED

Back in the 1970s, churches in Canada tended to be small and have limited vision. Often other pastors questioned our vision of "one church in multiple locations," but we chose to stay with the vision God had given our prayer group and to advance the future of our church. I prayed frequently, asking God to confirm the vision we had received and to give me a scriptural foundation for building our church. I firmly believe every vision needs to be confirmed and established on the Word of God.

During the weekend of our tenth anniversary as a church, we had a guest speaker named Dr. Dick Mills. God used Dr. Mills to forever settle the matter in our hearts and to confirm the future of our church.

It happened unexpectedly. Dr. Mills was napping in my car as I drove him from the airport to Red Deer. Suddenly he woke up and asked, "Mel, what is the vision of your church?"

I answered somewhat cautiously, "God gave us a vision of a big wheel, with a hub on fire and spokes on fire extending to the radius of the wheel. We believe our church will take the good news to many communities as one church in many locations."

Dick replied, "That is a biblical model for church growth and expansion. It's found in Acts 19. It's the Ephesians model." As we drove along the highway to Red Deer, he described the birth of the church in Ephesus, which was one church in many locations—just like ours.

When Paul arrived at Ephesus, he found twelve men who were followers of John the Baptist, and he led them to faith in Jesus and baptism in water and the Holy Spirit. Then they began regular meetings in the synagogue, and the group grew. After they were kicked out of the synagogue, they began a teaching center in a local lecture hall. Within two years, all of Asia Minor (modern-day Turkey) had heard the Word of God. There was a major spiritual movement, and the church was birthed throughout the province of Asia. Dr. Mills believed the church in Asia may have numbered 100,000 believers and was the largest church in the Roman Empire. He shared with me that they were "One church for the province of Asia."

This is not the only model for churches, nor is it the only God-given vision. Dr. Mills also explained the Jerusalem model of Acts 2, which was a "church for the city." Then he described the Antioch model, which was the self-governing, self-propagating model of church planting.

These are all great models, but the "one church" model was the one God had called our church to use as a pattern for church growth and multiplication. Today our vision is to plant a church location in every nation on Earth, preaching the good news of Jesus and making disciples in all nations.

Every church and every believer needs a God-given vision. Usually, the two work together: God gives a vision to church leadership, and He brings people to those churches who are divinely called and equipped to carry out the vision. Together, individuals and the church fulfill the vision God has given each of them.

Vision is what you see and what you believe. It becomes the foundation of your great future. God is calling you to stretch your thinking to see a bigger and greater vision for yourself and for His church in the world.

THINGS TO THINK ABOUT

1. Can you see the vision God has given your church leadership?

2. What kind of picture have you had in your past regarding God's church?

3. What part of God's vision have you been called to help fulfill?

DAY 4

Unstoppable
A church can never grow too big.

HOW BIG SHOULD a church grow? How big is too big? The answer is simple: *a church can never grow too big.* God's vision is for humanity, and as long as there are people who do not yet know Him, there is room for churches to grow. God's vision is beyond what you can reach for, beyond what you can count, and beyond what your hand can grasp.

When God called Abraham, He promised that his children would be greater in number than the stars of the sky and the sand of the sea (Genesis 15). God's promise for His church is the same. We are the children of Abraham and heirs according to the promise. Abraham believed the promise of God even when he had no children, and we as children of Abraham must have the same faith. There must be no limit to the number of people God can add to His church.

GOD HAS BIG PLANS

In the early years of our church, a traveling minister suggested the size of a local church should be the number of bones in the body, since the Bible refers to the church as the body of Christ. I did a little research and found babies are born with 270 bones; over time, some fuse together to form a mature skeletal structure of 206 bones. Misguided human concepts like this put artificial limits on the growth of God's church.

God's plan is that the church would grow, grow, and never stop growing until every person has received the message of Jesus and become part of a great local church. A church in a city can grow as large as the population of that city. A church in a country can grow as large as the population of that country. And the church in the world can grow to the population of the world.

The New Testament church was an unstoppable church. It began with 12 disciples following Jesus. At Pentecost, the Holy Spirit came upon 120 believers in an upper room, and the church was birthed. Peter preached to a crowd that gathered outside, and 3000 people who heard the good news responded and were saved. A few days later, another 5000 heard the message and were added to the church. The people met in the temple daily and from house to house, and the Lord added to their numbers continually. The church grew until it began to fill the city of Jerusalem with the doctrine of Christ.

With the rise of persecution, the church was scattered throughout the region. For example, Philip preached in Samaria, and the whole city turned to Christ as they witnessed the miracles he performed. On another occasion Peter raised a woman from the dead in Lydda, and the whole region of Sharon turned to the Lord. Soon after, Peter received a vision that he was to take the message to Cornelius, a Gentile (non-Jew). As a result the Gentile world began to open up to the good news of Jesus.

Believers fleeing persecution traveled to the city of Antioch and shared the good news of Jesus there. The church grew, and eventually Barnabas went to Antioch and took the newly converted Paul with him. They taught the believers there, and soon people outside the church began to call these believers *Christians* (Acts 11:26). Paul was sent by the Antioch church on three missionary journeys to plant churches in cities and towns throughout the Roman Empire. Eventually the entire empire became predominately Christian.

The church cannot be stopped. You can look at history and see times when the church strayed from its course and fell into political movements, military endeavors, and doctrinal error. But God has always brought the church back to its purpose and to purity. People like Martin Luther and others throughout history have stood on Scripture and directed believers back to God's goal for His church.

Even in my lifetime, I have seen amazing, encouraging changes in the church. Since the 1970s, I've seen megachurches begin to form around the world. Now thousands of churches worldwide are becoming multi-site, international churches. These churches can reshape and guide the influence of Christianity throughout the world.

The two greatest powers on earth are the *gospel* and the *church*. No human power—political, religious, military, or any other—can withstand these two forces. They were established by Jesus Himself. The Bible calls the gospel the "power of God to salvation" (Romans 1:16). Jesus told His disciples, "I will build my church, and all the powers of hell will not conquer it" (Matthew 16:18). A church that preaches the gospel cannot be stopped. Leaders, along with the people of God, simply need to learn how to stand until God's power prevails.

DIVISION CANNOT STOP THE UNSTOPPABLE CHURCH

In the early days of our church, when we had about seventy-five people in attendance, we went through a tough season. One of the leaders in the church didn't agree with our leadership structure, and he began to cause division and confusion. I remember a guest speaker giving me a word from God that if I would be faithful and endure tests of leadership and challenging times, the church would enter an incredible season of harvest. That was exactly what happened. There were some very difficult moments along the way, but God brought us through them.

Nearly twenty-five years later, another potential division began to form. The people at the heart of it were not bad people, but their vision and their opinions were at odds with where God was taking our church. The rest of the leadership team and I decided we needed to remain firm in our course. I recall saying to my wife, "I was made for this. We will get through this. Human strategies empowered by offenses and bitterness cannot prevail against the church Jesus is building."

It is always a challenge for leaders to unite strong, gifted people in a common vision that brings growth and increase to the church. It is not possible or necessary for everyone to agree all the time, but God is committed to using imperfect people to build His unstoppable church. He promised us this: "So no weapon that is used against you will defeat you. You will show that those who speak against you are wrong. These are the good things my servants receive. Their victory comes from me" (Isaiah 54:17 NCV).

DOCTRINAL DISSENSION CANNOT STOP THE UNSTOPPABLE CHURCH

One of the biggest challenges the New Testament church faced was false doctrine. What was true and what was false? Paul wrote a letter to the Colossians to clearly establish the doctrine of Christ. He wrote to the Galatians to establish their understanding of freedom and grace. He wrote to the leaders he mentored, Timothy and Titus, to help them correct the myths and false teachings that were being propagated in the churches.

The first council of the church in Jerusalem was held to establish the doctrine of salvation. After much disagreement and discussion, James brought the decision to a conclusion by establishing that salvation was by grace, not by obedience to the law.

The role of leadership is to preserve and teach sound doctrine, meaning beliefs that produce a healthy way of life (Titus 2:1). On a few occasions over the years, I have had to take a strong stand against false teachings that had subtly crept into the church.

POLITICAL OPPOSITION CANNOT STOP THE UNSTOPPABLE CHURCH

In some of our church locations in other nations, our leaders have faced great opposition. Their lives have been threatened, and some have been thrown in jail. In some places, if people are found with Bibles, they are put in prison for their faith.

In western nations like Canada, the opposition is less violent, but it is just as real. Often it revolves around the purchase of property or expansion of facilities. In Red Deer we faced unexpected, bizarre resistance when we attempted to purchase ten acres along a main highway in our area when the church was twenty years old. We had an agreement with the owner of the land, but both the city and the county opposed us fiercely. Neither wanted us to proceed because they both wanted control of the land. They were at odds with each other, and we were caught in the middle of a bureaucratic mess.

They would vote against our request, and I would appeal their decision, then they would vote against us again, and so on. On more than one occasion, I stood before our congregation and read aloud some of the prophetic words we had received about this step, and then I would lead them in prayer for favor. Then we would appeal again. This went on for three or four years.

Finally we went to the Alberta government appeal board. They sent representatives to our area to look into the matter, and they found no reason for the local government to deny our purchase. With a stroke of a pen, they granted us permission to continue with our development.

When authorities position themselves against God's will,

they will not prevail. The property became ours because we simply stood firm while God accomplished the impossible.

The church is unstoppable because God is unstoppable. *Financial lack* cannot stop the unstoppable church. *Human error and weakness* cannot stop the unstoppable church. *Impossible circumstances* cannot stop the unstoppable church. *Changes in leadership* cannot stop the unstoppable church. *Tragedy* cannot stop the unstoppable church. *Economic downturns* cannot stop the unstoppable church.

God promised that the whole earth will be filled with the glory of God (Isaiah 11:9). The church will prevail, and when time turns into eternity, we will be forever the eternal church, the people of God.

THINGS TO THINK ABOUT

1. What role can you play in the growth of your church?

2. How can you be an advocate of unity in your church so it can be unstoppable?

DAY 5

A *Small Church* with *Lots of People*
A *church that is big must always remain small.*

WHEN I WAS young, I could never have imagined a large, multi-site, international church. I was a small-town boy from a small church, and I grew up with small thinking. I was raised in a town of less than 5,000 people. The church my family attended was just 45 people. As a Bible college student, I took a summer pastoral position in a church with 30 people. Back then, a church with 300 people would have been considered a huge church. With such a small background, I never imagined I would plant and lead a church of thousands in multiple locations.

Something changed in me, though, when I made a trip to Asia in 1977 and visited a truly enormous church. Our congregation back home was only about 125 people at the time, so it was overwhelming to sit in the balcony during the service and see thousands of people pray and worship together. The sound was deafening, like "the sound of many waters," as the Bible says. Later in the week, I was amazed as I watched a hundred staff pastors come out of an early morning prayer meeting, go to their sectional offices, and make plans to visit people and organize cell group meetings in their sections of the city. That church eventually grew to over one million people.

Through that experience, I changed my mind about church size. I saw how large a church could grow and yet how small it could remain. The key was their thriving small group ministry.

I was inspired like never before to build a church that would have an impact in the world.

To be honest, a big church can be a little bit intimidating. It can make you feel small and almost lost in the crowd. You can't meet everyone or be friends with everyone. At the same time, however, being part of a big church can be incredibly exciting and beneficial. There are ministries for all ages and interests, the worship is usually amazing, and often the facilities are effective and beautiful. Even more importantly, the size and resources of the church mean it can reach many, many people for Jesus.

How can we enjoy the benefits of a large church while not making people feel lonely, lost, or disconnected? That is the challenge of any church that has a God-given vision to reach the world. *A church that is big must always remain small.*

Over the years we have developed a strong small group ministry at Home Church. I believe everyone needs to be part of a small group because these groups bring so many benefits to people's lives. For example:

1. In a small group, you find practical applications of the Word of God that is taught at the weekend services.
2. In a small group, you find people who believe with you for answered prayer.
3. In a small group, you find community.
4. In a small group, you learn to share your personal needs, thoughts, and feelings.
5. In a small group, you receive the love and support you need for the challenges you will face on life's journey.
6. In a small group, you are established in the beliefs of the body of Christ and find encouragement to continue in the faith.
7. In a small group, you grow to become the person God has called you to be.

When I travel I often ask people the question, "What percentage of your relationship with God is a result of personal prayer and reading the Bible, and what percentage is the result of your experience with God in church and in your small group?" The answer has been consistent in North America, Asia, and Africa: it's a 40/60 split. About 40% of people's relationship with God comes through personal, "alone" time with Him, and about 60% is connected to church.

That doesn't mean some institution or organization is the source of our relationship or that we need a mediator between God and us. Relationship with God is always personal. It means, however, that we often meet God while in community. Large gatherings, small groups, and even conversations with friends can all facilitate a deeper walk with Him.

It has always worked that way. God spoke to His people (through Moses) as a congregation when they gathered as the first church in the wilderness. Likewise He speaks to us today through the leaders He has established in His church, through corporate worship, and through other Jesus-followers.

Small groups can happen anywhere and with any age group. Recently a fourth-grade student in our church named Naomi received a devotional book for Christmas. She decided to use the book for a small group at her school. She called it the "Integrity Club."

Twice a week for five weeks, the group met during recess in the reading corner of their classroom. On Mondays Naomi taught the lesson, and on Thursdays she prepared games and activities connected to the lesson. Amazingly, an average of thirty children chose to miss recess to attend the group, and Naomi ended up leading seven of her classmates to Jesus!

In Naomi's words: "I was really happy that God placed that idea in my head...I felt like, *Yay! I did something good!* It was really exciting for me and probably really exciting for all those people."

Her story is so inspiring to me! It illustrates the need we all have for relationship and mutual encouragement. It also shows what can happen when someone, even a child, creates a place for others to thrive in community.

THINGS TO THINK ABOUT

1. What can you do in your church to build community?

2. What benefits have you experienced in your life from small groups?

Kacie's Story

I came to God very angry and in pain. I was burdened with bitterness, confusion, and hatred. The life I had lived up to that point was not what I would call ideal. I grew up in a split family, which wasn't terrible, but it wasn't superb, either. Being the youngest with a fairly large age gap between my next oldest sibling and me, I didn't quite feel like I fit into the family.

There seemed to be two sides to everything, and I was caught in between them. This caused me to start living two different lives. While on the outside I was acing school, people-pleasing, and sporting a "cookie-cutter" image, on the inside I was struggling to keep my head afloat. I started sneaking out and going to parties. I got involved with people much older than I, and I dove into the drugs and alcohol scene. I felt like I had different personalities. The greater the challenges became at home, the more I separated myself from the difficulties of reality and indulged in activities I would later realize would only curb my desires but never satisfy them.

Over the next four years, I lost four of the most important people in my life to suicide, along with many others to car crashes, overdoses, and illnesses. I reached a breaking point in my life where I was at the mercy of my emotions. I had no idea how to deal with or process the traumatic events that were taking place, and I felt hopeless and lost. I attempted suicide shortly after my boyfriend of two years took his own life, and I ended up in the children's hospital in Calgary, Alberta for three weeks.

In that confined space, I was forced to reconcile the hurt that I had *been carrying and to deal with the pain that festered inside. I cried out to God in anger. I blamed Him, and I questioned His sovereignty and love, wondering how He could kill so many people I loved and let me live in this life of hell. I realized I needed answers no human being could give me. I was searching for a higher level of understanding that could only come from God Himself (if He did truly exist).*

Once I left the hospital and went back to school, I was connected to a wonderful counselor who happened to be a Christian. She introduced me to a God of love and mercy who was not at all like the God I had believed in. This God was just as heartbroken as I was, and He called me by name in my pain. This was a love I had never known.

I began connecting with friends from school who had the same beliefs as me. I attended church off and on for a while, and then I began attending Home Church (Word of Life then) on Sunday evenings. I gave my life fully to God in February 2013, and I began Bible College in September 2013. My aunt and uncle walked me through salvation, and I moved in with them to start my faith journey. They have been a huge support and help to me in this new life I am privileged to live.

Since my salvation, life has not been easy. I have lost more people to suicide, overdose, and illness than most people have lost in their entire lives. Many attacks, whether emotional, physical or spiritual, have oppressed me at one time or another, but the God who lives in me is bigger than anything this world can throw at me. I wouldn't trade my life for anything. God has shown me that He has always seen me and loved me, and He loves me now.

My involvement in the church is very important to me. Serving my pastors, my city, my friends, my world, and my God is the best honor I could ever receive. I was baptized in November 2013, and my life has never been the same. Church grows me, feeds me spiritually, and gives me a greater family circle than I ever thought possible. I finally feel like I belong.

I BELIEVE
Foundations for your future

DAY 6

I *Believe in Jesus Christ*
Jesus is the eternal Son of God, our Savior.

SEVERAL YEARS AGO Heather and I had the opportunity to visit the Holy Land. We knew we didn't want to just hop on a tour bus and make the rounds with dozens of tourists. We wanted to explore it for ourselves and experience it at our own pace and in our own way. So we hired a local tour guide to take us around. He was a Palestinian Christian who could trace his heritage back to Bible times. His unique perspective, family history, and wealth of stories enriched our journey.

Our guide took us to Bethlehem, to Masada, and to the Dead Sea. We went to the city of Nazareth. My wife and I shared a kiss on the steps of the church where Jesus turned water into wine. In Capernaum, we could picture Jesus standing and declaring the Spirit of the Lord was upon Him to heal the broken-hearted and set the captives free. We saw the very tree Zacchaeus is believed to have climbed to get a better look at Jesus. We ascended the Mount of Olives, where Jesus prayed His great intercessory prayer, and we read the Beatitudes together as we looked out over the Sea of Galilee. We went to Caiphas' judgment hall and saw where Jesus stood before Pilate and was handed over to be crucified. We visited the empty garden tomb. We went to the Upper Room, where the disciples were first filled with the Holy Spirit.

One place in particular stood out to me on our trip: Caesarea Philippi. This site is near the border of Lebanon, about 250 kilometers from Jerusalem. Months before His death, Jesus took His disciples there and revealed to them, for the first time, He was indeed their Messiah.

Historically, Caesarea Philippi was a center of worship for the Greek god Pan. At one time there was a temple dedicated to Pan at this site, and for centuries people had gone there to worship him as the nourisher of life. There is a dark cave in the side of the mountain from which a spring of water emerges. This becomes the Banias River, a tributary of the Jordan River, which carries life-giving water to the land of Israel. In ancient times this cave was also known as the "Gate of Hades." There are stone gods carved into the cliff beside it, and in front there is a huge platform of rock.

When I looked at this scene, I could imagine Jesus there with His disciples. In this place of such historical and religious importance, He turned to them and asked the first of two important questions: "Who do people say I am?" (Matthew 16:13, paraphrased).

They replied, "Some say you are a prophet, or John the Baptist, or Elijah raised from the dead" (verse 14).

Everyone has an opinion about Jesus. Most people would agree He is the figurehead of Christianity; but beyond that, there is as much controversy today as there was when Jesus first asked the question. Some believe He is the living God, while others think He is just a long-dead prophet or teacher.

Jesus clearly claimed to be God. He said, "Before Abraham was even born, I am" (John 8:58), a reference to the name God gave Himself when He revealed Himself to Israel in Egypt. He said He was the Son of God, which made Him equal to the Father.

These claims infuriated the religious leaders, and they had heated debates in the temple square. Eventually their anger led them to crucify Jesus. They didn't believe that the man standing in front of them was the Son of God, even though they had seen Him turn water into wine, heal a man who had been born blind, and raise Lazarus from the dead. Jesus had demonstrated that He was God in the flesh, yet they refused to believe He was who He claimed and proved Himself to be.

When Jesus and His disciples visited Caesarea Philippi and saw the religious symbols that were as hollow as the cave that held them, Jesus asked them, "Who do you say I am?"

Peter boldly declared, "You are the Messiah, the son of the living God" (Matthew 16:16).

Defining Christ's place in your heart and life is imperative. You become a follower of Jesus Christ when you firmly believe in Him and confess Him as Lord.

Jesus took His disciples to Caesarea Philippi to establish them in their faith, since by their confession they recognized He was the Christ, the Son of the living God. In that moment, the disciples made clear they believed Jesus was God. Their faith was rooted and real. Peter said on another occasion, "We believe, and we know you are the Holy One of God" (John 6:69).

MORE THAN A MERE MAN

Throughout the centuries, many have attempted to water down the identity of Jesus. They have tried to make Him no more than a human. The New Testament deals with this issue clearly.

The apostle Paul

The book of Colossians was written to believers in the New Testament period to firmly declare who Jesus is because, just like today, people were trying to convince them He was less than God. Paul wrote:

Christ is the visible image of the invisible God. He existed before anything was created and is supreme over all creation.

... For God in all his fullness was pleased to live in Christ, and through him God reconciled everything to himself. He made peace with everything in heaven and on earth by means of Christ's blood on the cross.
(Colossians 1:15, 19-20)

The apostle John

In the beginning the Word already existed. The Word was with God, and the Word was God. ... So the Word became human and made his home among us. He was full of unfailing love and faithfulness. And we have seen his glory, the glory of the Father's one and only Son.
(John 1:1, 14)

We proclaim to you the one who existed from the beginning, whom we have heard and seen. We saw him with our own eyes and touched him with our own hands. He is the Word of life. This one who is life itself was revealed to us, and we have seen him. And now we testify and proclaim to you that he is the one who is eternal life. He was with the Father, and then he was revealed to us.
(1 John 1-2)

The book of Hebrews

The book of Hebrews was written to Jewish Christians who had been scattered in times of famine and persecution. One of its main themes is that Jesus is greater than anyone or anything else.

He is greater than the angels (Hebrews 1:5-14). He is greater than Moses, who gave Israel the Law, which included the Ten Commandments and other religious rules Israel was required to follow (3:1-6). He is greater than Aaron and the priesthood of the Old Testament (4:1-10). He is greater than Abraham and the heroes of Jewish history (7:1-22). He is a greater sacrifice and He established a greater covenant than the Law (9:11-28).

Jesus is bigger and greater and better than anything life or the Law could offer. He is God and holds the highest office. He handed himself over to sin and death so that He could win the victory over both. Now He rules and reigns over all.

The controversy that stirred the temple square must be resolved in your heart. How would you answer Jesus' question? Who do you say He is? Can you say with Peter, "You are the Christ, the Son of the Living God"?

Jesus is our Savior and Redeemer, the Lord of the universe, and the foundation of our lives. It is this confession that sets us free from sin, anchors us to the Rock of Ages, and builds the church.

THINGS TO THINK ABOUT

1. What beliefs have you had about Jesus in the past?

2. Why is it important to believe Jesus is more than a man—He is God?

3. What changes have you made to make Jesus the foundation of your life?

I *Believe* in the Bible

*The Bible—nothing more and nothing less—is the
inspired Word of God.*

WHEN I WAS a young pastor, I had to decide if I really believed in
the Bible. I encountered people, including ministers, who believed the Bible *contains* the words of God but is not *actually* and
entirely the Word of God. They believed the books of the Bible
were full of mystical stories that did not really happen as recorded in Scripture. For many of them, the accounts of creation,
David and Goliath, and Jonah and the big fish were simply fairy
tales, a series of stories grouped together to communicate a moral.

As I studied the Bible, I concluded it is much more than a
collection of fables or helpful teachings. It is the Word of God,
given by God as a gift to humanity. The Holy Spirit inspired
and directed its creation from cover to cover. Every word is
true and relevant to my life. I decided I would believe nothing
more and nothing less. I made it the guideline for my faith, and
I have never regretted it.

The Bible was written over a period of sixteen hundred
years by thirty-nine different authors inspired by the Holy
Spirit. It is a book of history, poetry, prophecy, and factual accounts of people on their journeys of faith. It describes the failure of humanity and God's wonderful plan of salvation through
Jesus Christ.

WHY I LOVE THE BIBLE

I love the Bible because it "tells it like it is." It describes the good, the bad, and the ugly. It doesn't just stick to telling rosy success stories and tales of victory, but it includes the nasty stuff too—like how Adam and Eve fell into sin and how mankind has been failing God and each other ever since. It includes both good and evil. It teaches about both right and wrong.

Because the Bible is inspired, honest, and complete, it is the surest foundation for faith and conduct. When we read the Bible, we establish truth for our lives. We learn how to make good decisions and how to avoid making bad ones.

I love the Bible because it is all about God. It is His story. His attributes are on display, and His character is unveiled. The more we read about Him, the more we love who He is, and the more we want to become like Him.

I love the Bible because it is a book of God's promises. The Bible describes several covenants God made with His children long ago and the covenants He made with us too.

The Old Testament describes the many ways God fulfilled His promises to people like Noah, Abraham, Esther, David, Elijah, and others. In the New Testament, we see how God fulfilled His promise to save us from sin and give us abundant life. He gave us His only Son, Jesus, so whoever believes in Him would not spend eternity without God but would have everlasting life with Him. The entire Bible points to Jesus and to God's plan of redemption through Him.

I love the Bible because it teaches us how to live healthy, wise, successful lives. It sets the standard for daily living. It instructs us how to have good marriages and families; it describes the relationships we are to have with others; it teaches us how to do business and influence our communities; it describes best practices for work; and it shows us how to be great leaders.

THE BIBLE IN YOUR LIFE

The Bible relates to every area of life. It's our answer book and instruction manual. The apostle Paul put it this way: "Every part of Scripture is God-breathed and useful one way or another—showing us truth, exposing our rebellion, correcting our mistakes, training us to live God's way. Through the Word we are put together and shaped up for the tasks God has for us" (2 Timothy 3:16 MSG).

Since the Word of God guides our decisions, it's good to spend time with it and in it. It's important to meditate on it and to talk about it. Let it take root in your heart and transform you. When you focus on God's Word and do what it says, it has the power to clean, restore, and free you.

God told Joshua, "And don't for a minute let this Book of the revelation be out of mind. Ponder and meditate on it day and night, making sure you practice everything written in it. Then you'll get where you're going; then you'll succeed" (Joshua 1:8 MSG).

James wrote, "So get rid of all of the filth and evil in your lives, and humbly accept the word God has planted in your hearts, for it has the power to save your souls. But don't just listen to God's word. You must do what it says. Otherwise, you are only fooling yourselves" (James 1:21-22).

THE BIBLE, THE WHOLE BIBLE, AND NOTHING BUT THE BIBLE

Home Church is clearly established on the foundation of Scripture. Every book, chapter, and verse of the Bible is important. The New Testament must be interpreted based on the foundation of the Old Testament. The words of Peter, Paul, and James complement each other. Jesus' teachings must be understood in the context of the entire Bible.

47

Unfortunately, some people pick and choose what is important and what is secondary to them. They lay aside parts of the Bible as less important than others. Over the years I've met some people who just focus on the Ten Commandments and the Law, while others only read the New Testament, and yet others are "red-letter Christians" who only care about what Jesus said. I believe we should be people who believe the whole thing, cover to cover, Genesis to Revelation. I believe "All Scripture is given by inspiration of God and is profitable" (2 Timothy 3:16 NKJV).

It is also important to refrain from adding to the Bible. Historically, the church has on occasion made the mistake of adding dogmas, decrees, and traditions to Scripture and then labeling these divine truth. In the modern day charismatic movement, extra-biblical "revelations" of some apostles, prophets, and teachers have caused great conflict and brought error into the church. Our opinions, our practices, and our church cultures never have the same level of authority as Scripture. When God speaks to us, it will always line up with the Bible. Everything we do and teach must be evaluated in light of what God's Word says.

Every follower of Jesus should accept that the Bible is the inspired Word of God and the final authority for faith and practice. We should read the entire Bible and live by the principles found in its pages. We cannot have real faith in God without having real faith in Scripture.

THINGS TO THINK ABOUT

1. Is the Bible your standard of truth? Is everything in your world filtered through the Word of God?

2. How has the Bible helped shape your life and decisions?

Jodi's Story

After a six-hour radical hysterectomy, I was told I had ovarian cancer. Three weeks later, doctors informed me it was stage 3 ovarian cancer and my only hope was radical chemotherapy and radiation. To be exact, they said that with chemotherapy and radiation treatment, I had a 1% chance to live for a year; without it, I had a 0% chance to live even for a year.

I felt like they didn't have answers for me and I should not complete their suggested treatments, but I knew Jesus had all the answers. Jesus' Word says that by His stripes, I am completely healed (Isaiah 53:5 and 1 Peter 2:24). Jesus' Word says no weapon formed against me shall prosper (Isaiah 54:17). Jesus said in Jeremiah 29:11 that He has plans for my life—plans to prosper me and give me great health and a great future. Jesus said to commit all my plans to Him and He would make them succeed (Proverbs 16:3). Jesus said that if I believed, He would heal me; that my only job was to believe with all my heart and He would move this mountain.

So I started on a journey of cleansing my mind, body, and soul. But I knew only Jesus could guide and direct me through this process. Every day, I went to God's Word. That was my medication, and I knew there would be no side effects.

After three months I was checked and my blood work looked pretty good; however, iron levels were low and thyroid levels were low, so I had to work on that. Again, every day, I went to God's Word and spoke His Word over my circumstance. His Word says nothing is impossible (Matthew 19:26), even though the doctors said they couldn't do anything for me.

I memorized Scripture, and God's Word went from my head to my heart. I believed what He said: if you have faith as a mustard seed, you will move whatever mountain you need to move (Matthew 17:20). I looked at my diagnosis as a mountain that God could totally move. I thanked God several times a day for my healing. My focus had to be completely on God's Word so that I had no doubt He would heal my body. There were moments and days when I felt like I couldn't do this, but with an army of friends and family cheering me on, encouraging me, and telling me I could do it, I would quickly shake off defeat and move forward.

After seven months I was given a clean bill of health, and I have never looked back. I still thank Jesus for my healing and great health. Jesus is our ultimate healer. He will guide all our steps if we let Him. We just need to trust that every second of every minute of every day, He has our back, and He wants us to be well and prosper in every avenue of life.

DAY 8

I Believe in the Gospel
The gospel is good news.

WHEN I WAS seven years old, I attended an evangelistic crusade in the city of Estevan, in southern Saskatchewan, Canada. I remember buses and cars picking up children from all the schools in the community and taking us to the afternoon children's services. Every day I sat and listened attentively to the children's evangelist as she told the stories of creation, of the fall of Adam and Eve in the garden, and of God's wonderful plan of salvation. She described Jesus' birth in a stable, His life and miracles, and His death upon the cross for our sins.

On Thursday afternoon of the crusade, the evangelist placed a big heart on the board and a picture of Jesus knocking on the door of the heart. She said, "Boys and girls, if you will invite Jesus into your heart, He will come in and live forever with you."

At the invitation, I lifted my hand, then walked forward with scores of children. We prayed a prayer to accept Christ, then we all received a Bible as a gift. I remember knowing that day that I was saved. I had an inner peace in my heart, even at that age, and I had faith I had received the gift of eternal life. Since then, I have come to understand more fully the salvation I received that day, and I have the assurance I am eternally saved.

The gospel is good news! God became a man in the person of Jesus Christ. He lived a perfect, sinless life and died upon the cross so we could receive forgiveness from our sins. He rose again from the dead on the third day and is seated at the right hand of the Father. He offers the gift of eternal life to everyone who repents of their sin and believes the gospel.

JESUS IS GOOD NEWS

The word *gospel* in Greek is *evangelion*, which literally means "good news." The fact the gospel is good news was apparent every time Jesus preached. One day, at the local synagogue, He asked for an Old Testament scroll and began to read the good news to His community. He read this portion from Isaiah:

> The Spirit of the Lord is on me, because he has anointed me to proclaim good news to the poor. He has sent me to proclaim freedom for the prisoners and recovery of sight for the blind, to set the oppressed free, to proclaim the year of the Lord's favor.
> (Luke 4:18-19 NIV)

The Year of Jubilee was a Jewish tradition, and Jesus' hearers would have understood the reference to "the year of the Lord's favor." During Jubilee, slaves were set free, debts were canceled, and new life began. Jesus was announcing that in Him, new life was granted, the debt of sin was canceled, and true freedom had begun.

This was good news to a country that had lived under the Roman rule of the Caesars for many years. In Jesus, they could find freedom from oppression, sin, sickness, and poverty. They could enjoy the blessing and provision of God.

Jesus said on another occasion, "I have come that they may have life, and that they may have it more abundantly" (John 10:10 NKJV). The gospel of Jesus is first and foremost salvation from sins, but that salvation includes the full, blessed, abundant life God has for us now. Abundant life begins here on earth and finds its ultimate fulfillment in heaven.

At Home Church, we boldly declare the Word of God in all our Sunday services, teaching people how to live the abundant life God designed for us in their families, workplaces, and communities.

What is the good news of Jesus?
1. God became a man in the person of Jesus Christ.
2. He lived a perfect life.
3. He died on the cross in our place.
4. He rose triumphantly from the grave.
5. He is at the right hand of God as the Lord of the universe.
6. He offers to everyone who repents and believes the good news of the gift of eternal life.

Our good news is unique. Most religions, belief systems, and philosophies teach that you get what you deserve. Jesus came to give us what we could never deserve. The Bible says, "God made him who had no sin to be sin for us, so that in him we might become the righteousness of God" (2 Corinthians 5:21 NIV). Jesus did for us what we could never do for ourselves.

THE GOOD NEWS IS FOR EVERYONE

John 3:16, one of the most famous verses in the Bible, says this: "For God so loved the world that he gave his one and only Son, that whoever believes in him shall not perish but have eternal life" (NIV). Anyone and everyone has access to God through Jesus. Receiving and believing the gospel is a personal experience, and it is necessary to enter the kingdom of God.

Jesus referred to this experience as being "born again" (John

3:3). In other words, the good news of the message of Jesus is that we have new life in Him. We are a new people, and our old way of thinking and living has disappeared. Paul wrote in 2 Corinthians 5:17, "This means that anyone who belongs to Christ has become a new person. The old life is gone; a new life has begun!" Once, we were trapped in sin, bound by poverty, limited by sickness, held back by addictions, and hindered by guilt; but now, we are a new creation in Jesus, and He gives us new life. That is good news!

Not only are we the recipients of good news, we are also the bearers of it. It is the calling and privilege of every person who has been born again to share the good news with others on every possible occasion. Everyone needs Jesus, and everyone needs a home!

THINGS TO THINK ABOUT

1. Why is the gospel good news?

2. Who in your world needs to hear the good news of Jesus? Are you regularly sharing the good news with family, friends, neighbors, and business associates?

Doug's Story

In October of 2011 my dad and I loaded my car onto a trailer along with my tools and a suitcase full of clothing. My wife, Ashley, and I were separated with two children. I had been living in Kelowna, British Columbia, but had taken a job in Red Deer, Alberta. I figured if I could make more money, it would solve all our problems.

As we pulled into Red Deer on a Sunday, I searched the internet for a place to live. The first person I called told me, "I'm just finishing up at church, and then I can show you the place."

I told my dad, "He goes to church. I won't be living there." But an hour later, I found myself moving into his place. Every Saturday night over the next several weeks, my new roommate, Brayden, would invite me to go to church with him the following morning. I remember having several conversations about church and how I believed in God but not religion. Brayden's house was always full of people coming and going, and there was always a "different" atmosphere about it. Everyone was always very kind and accepting of me.

One Saturday night after everyone had left, I came out of my room and sat on the couch opposite Brayden. He invited me to go to church in the morning like he always did. This night was different, though. He pushed a little more than usual. He made some small talk, and then he told me, "You don't need to know everything before you believe, and you don't need to believe before you belong."

That statement caught me off guard. My whole life, I never really felt like I belonged to anything. I struggled with suicidal depression from the age of fourteen. I would drink until I blacked out; I smoked pot to relieve stress; I became a workaholic. I did anything I could to fill the time and to keep the demons in my head quiet. I never told anyone about it—not even my wife. I just kept bottling everything up. It drove a wedge between my wife and me as well as my family. They knew something was wrong, but I would never admit it. Not a day went by that I didn't think about suicide.

After two months of living with Brayden, I finally caved in and agreed to go to church—as long as we didn't sit on the front row. But of course, we did sit on the front row, to the far right of the sanctuary. People were friendly and welcoming; the music was loud. It was a lot different than I had known church to be. The pastor, Jachin Mullen, got up and spoke about building your foundation on the rocks and not on the sand. The more he spoke, the more I felt like he was talking directly to me. Everyone in the room seemed to vanish. I went home that day feeling different. I read the gospels of John and Matthew. It felt like some weight had been lifted from my shoulders.

That Friday night, I came home from work to an email from my wife asking for a divorce. She wasn't sure what to do anymore to make me happy and was tired of trying. We had been separated for four months at this point but emotionally distant for around seven months. I told her about the depression, I told her I had gone to church, and I asked her to give me some time. She agreed. The following Sunday, November 13, I gave my life to Christ. I'll never forget the weight that lifted as the tears streamed down my face.

I shared my journey with my wife. Every day I would message her letting her know what I had read or heard. I sent her Christian songs that I thought were good. It was like I had been given new life.

Christmas came around, and I had saved enough money to fly home to see Ashley and the kids as well as my family. Things felt weird. There was a tension around my family, and I kept to myself, not sure how my family would feel about me being a Christian.

I flew back to Red Deer on December 27. I spent New Year's evening with a bunch of friends from the church. On January 2, I received a message from a guy stating he was emotionally involved with my wife. I was heartbroken. Everything I had accomplished in the two months prior came crashing down on me. I sought council from leaders in the church, and I decided to sell my car in order to move my wife and kids to Red Deer so we could try to make things work. I sold my car for exactly what it cost to cover my damage deposit and first month's rent.

To my surprise, Ashley came to church with me right away. She ended up giving her life to Jesus at a service for young adults called The Collective, led by Pastor Steven Schwartz. He had been speaking on the book of Ruth. Two weeks later, during a Sunday night service, Pastor Jachin was speaking on the Blood of Christ. He was using a twenty-foot scarlet ribbon to illustrate. As he weaved through the aisles and seats, he came to where Ashley and I were sitting and stopped. He handed my wife the scarlet ribbon and prayed over our marriage. That night Ashley made the decision to get baptized. We still have the scarlet ribbon hung above our bed.

We got baptized together on February 19, 2012; we renewed our wedding vows on July 6, 2013; and we had our third child on March 31, 2014. We've been married now for nine years and together for thirteen.

Looking back, the Gospel literally saved my life. God's divine providence is woven into our testimony. We've had the honor of being able to share our story and see other families saved. Our path hasn't been easy. We've had highs and lows, but knowing that God is ultimately in control of every situation makes the struggles of life easier to deal with.

This is the good news: knowing that God not only loved Ashley and me enough to repair our broken marriage, but He gave His only Son for it.

I *Believe in the* Holy Spirit

The Holy Spirit is a real person, and we have real experiences with Him.

I WILL NEVER forget the night at a Christian camp in Southern Saskatchewan when I experienced being filled with the Holy Spirit. Several years prior, when I was seven years of age, I had come to know Christ as my Savior, and I was born again. However, it wasn't until I was eleven that I received the experience referred to in Scripture as the "baptism with the Holy Spirit" or being "filled with the Holy Spirit."

It was about eleven o'clock on a Thursday night, and several hundred people were praying around an old wooden altar at the front of the auditorium. Suddenly we became aware of the tangible presence of the Holy Spirit in the room, and many of us began to speak in other languages as the Spirit gave us words to speak. I remember the unexplainable, beautiful gushings from the heart as my mouth began to say words I didn't understand. The experience was similar to Acts 2, when the believers gathered together in Jerusalem to receive the promise Jesus had given them: "You will receive power when the Holy Spirit comes upon you. And you will be my witnesses . . ." (Acts 1:8).

That night was the beginning of an empowerment that would change my life forever. It would send me to preach the good news of Jesus, train leaders, and establish the church in nations around the world. I experienced and understood what Jesus said when He told His disciples to wait "until the Holy Spirit comes and fills you with power from heaven" (Luke 24:49).

The Bible teaches that this amazing experience is available for every Christian. After the initial experience of Pentecost in Acts 2, Peter stood before thousands of people and said, "Each of you must repent of your sins and turn to God, and be baptized in the name of Jesus Christ for the forgiveness of your sins. Then you will receive the gift of the Holy Spirit. This promise is to you, to your children, and to those far away—all who have been called by the Lord our God" (Acts 2:38-39). In other words, this promise is for *everyone* who believes in Jesus.

TWO EXPERIENCES

God's plan for each of us as we enter His kingdom includes two wonderful experiences with the Holy Spirit. These experiences were present from the very birth of the church in Acts 2.

EXPERIENCE 1: *Salvation, including repentance and forgiveness*

When you receive Christ into your life, you are instantly and wholly saved and forgiven. At this moment, the Holy Spirit enters your heart and marks you as a child of God. Your sins are washed away, and you begin to walk in freedom and in a new relationship with Christ.

EXPERIENCE 2: *The baptism with the Holy Spirit*

The filling of the Holy Spirit is an experience of empowerment that leads you into a closer relationship with the third person of the Trinity, the Holy Spirit.

We often use the term "baptism" to refer to this experience because of the words of Jesus to His disciples just before He returned to heaven: "Do not leave Jerusalem until the Father sends you the gift he promised, as I told you before. John baptized with water, but in just a few days you will be baptized with the Holy Spirit" (Acts 1:4-5).

A REAL PERSON

The Holy Spirit is a real person, not an impersonal force. We can have a personal relationship with the Spirit. We read in 2 Corinthians 13:14 about "the communion of the Holy Spirit," which refers to the fellowship or relationship we have with the Spirit.

The Spirit dwells in us from the point of salvation. He establishes Christ in our hearts, and we become the temple of the Holy Spirit. As we walk in this new relationship, the Holy Spirit becomes our personal guide, teacher, companion, and friend, and He even shows us things that are yet to come (John 14, 16).

The Holy Spirit is *in us and with us*, and the Holy Spirit *empowers us*. These are two distinct aspects of the work of the Spirit in our daily lives.

In and with:
The Holy Spirit comes into us and abides in us, starting at the point of salvation. He lives in our hearts by faith, and He identifies us as children of God. As we go about our daily activities, there are times we become aware of His presence leading and guiding us in the daily decisions of life.

Empower:
The Holy Spirit gives us the energy and strength to fulfill the tasks Jesus has called us to accomplish. This is one of the results of the baptism with the Holy Spirit.

A relationship with the Holy Spirit is like a relationship with another human being. As you get to know a person better, you come into a closer, deeper, and more intimate relationship. That person becomes known to you, and you become known to him or her. A similar thing happens in our walk with the Spirit. The more time we spend with Him, the better we get to know Him and the closer our relationship becomes.

Jesus Himself invites us into this wonderful two-fold relationship with the Holy Spirit. He said in John 7:38,

> Anyone who is thirsty may come to me! Anyone who believes in me may come and drink! For the Scriptures declare, "Rivers of living water will flow from his heart." (When he said "living water," he was speaking of the Spirit, who would be given to everyone believing in him. But the Spirit had not yet been given, because Jesus had not yet entered into his glory.)

FILLED AND EMPOWERED

The Holy Spirit comes to dwell in us at the point of our salvation, and He empowers us when we experience the filling with the Holy Spirit. These two experiences—the indwelling of the Spirit and the filling of the Spirit—are distinct, as we discussed above.

In the Old Testament, the empowerment of the Holy Spirit was a rare event reserved for a few people. For example, the Holy Spirit came upon King Saul and caused him "to prophesy...and be turned into another man" (1 Samuel 10:6 ESV). David was anointed with oil to become the king of Israel, and the Holy Spirit came upon him (1 Samuel 16:13). The Spirit came mightily upon Samson on many occasions, resulting in the deliverance of Israel from bondage: including lifting city gates from their hinges and bringing down a building by knocking over the columns holding it up, all in the strength of the Spirit (Judges 14-16).

In the New Testament, the Holy Spirit is available to all. We see a clear biblical illustration of being filled and empowered by the Holy Spirit in Acts 19:1-6. Paul asked a group of twelve believers at Ephesus, "Did you receive the Holy Spirit when you believed?" (verse 2). Since they did not understand what it meant to be baptized in water in the name of Jesus or baptized in the Holy Spirit, He took them down to the river, baptized them in water, and they were filled with the Holy Spirit and began to speak in tongues and prophesy.

This unique, separate experience of the baptism with the Holy Spirit is also well illustrated when Philip the evangelist preached the Word of God in the city of Samaria (Acts 8:4-17). The city responded to the message, and many were baptized in the name of Jesus. The leaders in Jerusalem heard that Samaria had received the Word of God, and they sent Peter to lay hands on the new believers so they would receive the experience of baptism in the Spirit.

Experiencing the Holy Spirit is important for every follower of Jesus. The Spirit wants to empower us so we can fulfill the tasks God has called us to do.

A few years ago, Susan, a staff member in our outreach ministry, expressed frustration about a particular prayer need. She felt God had put someone on her heart to pray for, but she didn't know what to pray. Her pastor suggested she pray in the Spirit. Susan was silent, because she didn't know how. In the weeks leading up to this conversation, I had been preaching a sermon series on the Holy Spirit, so she had heard about speaking in tongues, but she had never experienced it.

Her pastor and his wife offered to pray for her after the next Sunday service. She came to church, listened to the message about the Holy Spirit, and decided she wanted to receive the baptism in the Spirit. When I gave the call for prayer at the end, she walked to the front of the auditorium and went straight to her pastors. They prayed for her and encouraged her to just open her mouth and begin talking. Instantly she started speaking in tongues.

She told us later it was "an effortless experience." She now says she feels closer to God than ever before, and she is so excited about being able to pray more effectively for others and for herself.

I love that word "effortless." You don't have to do anything special to receive the baptism with the Holy Spirit. The Spirit is a gift. You do not have to work for His presence. You receive His filling by faith. Simply invite the Holy Spirit to fill you and empower you.

As God baptizes you with His Spirit, you will be empowered to do His will. You will know and experience the power of the Holy Spirit. The Spirit is available to everyone. Will you receive Him?

THINGS TO THINK ABOUT:

1. Have you received the baptism with the Holy Spirit? If so, describe the experience.

2. Why do you need the Holy Spirit to empower you?

3. How does the Holy Spirit help you in your day-to-day life?

I *Believe* in the *Church*
The church is believers assembled with structure and purpose.

A FEW YEARS ago Heather and I visited a world-renowned cathedral in another part of the world. We paid our entrance fee and rented handheld recorders to listen to the audio tour. As we walked from room to room, the recorded voice informed us about the background of the building.

Construction had begun over one hundred years earlier and would be finished during this century. The famous architect who designed the church donated millions of dollars from his personal wealth, believing this great edifice would help pay for his eternal salvation. The audio guide also informed us our entrance fee and recorder rental would help reduce our own time in purgatory.

As we toured the incredible edifice, we felt in awe of the architecture, but we didn't feel the presence of God that we have so often experienced in our church in Red Deer. There was no sense of the love of God, no relationship with Him, no expression of intimacy and trust.

I don't mean to criticize the beliefs of others, and I understand there are different expressions of faith and relationship with God. Certainly some of those visiting that edifice must have felt inspired to know God, or at least to worship and fear Him. But as I looked around at the hundreds of tourists visiting the cathedral, I wondered how many of them believed this is what church is all about: beautiful architecture, steeples, stained glass windows, murals, giving money, and doing good works to appease a cold, distant God.

Partly in reaction to the institutionalization of church and religion, there was a movement at the turn of the twenty-first century to downplay and dismantle the church as an organization. I remember sitting with about four hundred ministers in Dallas, Texas in 2008 and listening to a minister say, "We must redefine the *ecclesia*" (the Greek word for church). A few weeks later, I was at a television station for an interview on a Christian television show, and the receptionist remarked, "Pastor, the church has really changed, hasn't it? We don't need to go to a building or a service anymore. Church can be a coffee shop, a car dealership, or anywhere Christians are."

Again, I don't mean to be critical of other people's opinions, but that receptionist's view of the church doesn't do justice to the biblical definition of church. Yet, it is wrong to define church as a building or cathedral, but it is also a mistake to dismiss local churches as unnecessary. We need to rediscover the true Bible definition of the church. Church includes form and structure, but it is much more than that.

THE NEW TESTAMENT CHURCH

The church in the book of Acts was a united people of God who met together in the temple and from house to house (Acts 2:46). When believers came together, they became the church. Their gatherings—both large and small—were very important to them.

The church of Acts was a real church with tangible, physical expression. It was more than buildings or structure, but it included physical meeting places and organization. Their gatherings involved worship, prayer, the teaching of the Word, the expression of spiritual gifts, and the presence of God.

Often, we use the terms "universal church" and "local church" to distinguish between two different meanings of the term. The universal church refers to all believers, everywhere, throughout all time. It is spiritual and intangible. Local churches, on the other hand, are concrete, tangible communities of believers who meet together regularly to worship God.

Paul wrote his letters to specific congregations of people. These local churches were groups of people who, under the guidance of their leaders, were fulfilling God's purpose of reaching people in their communities with the good news of Jesus.

Today there are churches all over the globe. Each local church is an expression of the universal church, which is the body of Christ. There are many individual churches, and each is part of the one invisible, global, and timeless church, with Jesus as the Head. It is important we realize the significance of the local church we are a part of, while at the same time valuing the entire body of Christ with its many different expressions.

THE CHURCH IN THE WILDERNESS

The first example and definition of the church is found in the amazing story of the children of Israel when they came out of bondage in Egypt and journeyed toward the Promised Land. Scripture calls them "the church in the wilderness" (Acts 7:38). Three million people became the people of God, one church on a journey together toward the promises of God.

The nation of Israel was a picture of God's people. Moses' leadership of Israel in the wilderness not only modeled what leadership is meant to look like, but it defined what the church is and should be. The Israelites were delivered from the bondage and tyranny of Egypt. They experienced a corporate relationship with God and received the Ten Commandments, which became their guide for life in the wilderness. They had a leadership structure with captains of thousands, hundreds, fifties, and tens.

The congregation in the wilderness was structured for forward movement, and they moved together as one people toward their promised land. God's promises, provision, and presence were theirs to enjoy as the family of God.

Just as the church in the wilderness experienced relationship with God, leadership, order, structure, and a future of promise, so the church today is called to experience these things. The church is not some mystical, ethereal concept, but a real group of people who experience God's redemptive salvation power and are freed from the bondage and tyranny of a sinful past. The true church is a people called out of the world and united as the people of God.

The church in the wilderness illustrates five facets of God's church. It is the *called out*, *gathered*, *assembled*, *equipped*, and *sent* people of God.

1. We are the called-out people of God.

Moses stretched out his rod with God-given authority, and the people of Israel were freed from the bondage and tyranny of Egypt. This is a picture of what happens to us when we find Christ as our Savior and Lord. Jesus saved us and called us out of darkness into His glorious light. Now that we know Jesus, we are delivered from the power and punishment of sin. The tyranny of Satan and the power of the world no longer have a grip on our lives. We are called out of the world and into a glorious relationship with Jesus.

2. We are the gathered people of God.

Israel was an estimated three million people strong when Moses led the nation into the wilderness. They were twelve tribes with little structure. Then God began to give Moses instructions that brought order to the multitude: the Ten Commandments, the tabernacle, and subdivisions and appointment of leaders within tribes. The book of Numbers describes this massive process of turning a crowd into a congregation, a term used over 130 times from Exodus to Deuteronomy.

3. We are the assembled people of God.

Around the tabernacle, where the presence of God resided, God directed Moses to place the tribes in a specific order. They became an assembled people, organized and structured so they could move toward the Promised Land. The Old Testament calls the people of God an "assembly" nearly 150 times. The New Testament refers to "the assembly of God's firstborn children, whose names are written in heaven" (Hebrews 12:23).

The term *assembly* contains the idea of belonging and coming together; diverse parts are assembled and fit together under the direction of Jesus and through leaders God has appointed. An assembled gathering can be the smallest group that meets in the name of the Lord or a megachurch that meets with thousands of people. Just as a house is not a complete house until the foundation is laid and all the parts are in place, so a church is not a complete church until it is built and becomes the dwelling place of God.

4. We are the equipped and trained people of God.

In the wilderness the people were trained in the principles of Scripture about how to live and follow God. They trained for warfare and prepared to fight battles so they could conquer when they entered the Promised Land.

In the same way, the New Testament presents the church as a resource for equipping and training. It is not just a place where people go through the motions of prayer and spirituality, but a place where children, youth, and adults are trained to be the people of God on earth, people who know how to win spiritual battles.

5. We are the sent people of God.

God had a mission for Israel: to establish His rule and authority in the Promised Land. Israel was sent by God with a purpose. In the New Testament, the Greek word for "sent" is *apostolis*, from which we get the word "apostolic." Paul and Barnabas, for example, were "sent out by the Holy Spirit" (Acts 13:4), and they went with the blessing and authority of church leaders to plant churches throughout the Roman empire. As Christians and churches, we are sent on a mission to proclaim the good news and make followers of Jesus.

FIVE PICTURES OF THE CHURCH

The book of Ephesians uses five metaphors to describe the church. Each metaphor is a picture that communicates certain facets of what the church is to be.

1. The Church is God's house.

"Together, we are his house, built on the foundation of the apostles and the prophets. And the cornerstone is Christ Jesus himself" (Ephesians 2:20).

The great mystery of the church is this: when we come together as living stones, built on the foundation of the apostles and prophets and aligned with the cornerstone (Christ Himself), God comes by His Holy Spirit to dwell within us.

2. The Church is Christ's body.

"We will speak the truth in love, growing in every way more and more like Christ, who is the head of his body, the church" (Ephesians 4:15).

Christ is the Head of His church, and we are all connected members, joined together like a human body. All the parts are connected and held together by the love of God. Just as the human body has parts that work together for the proper functioning of the body, so His church is a living structure that works together as the body of Christ in the world.

3. The Church is God's family.

"So now you Gentiles are no longer strangers and foreigners. You are citizens along with all of God's holy people. You are members of God's family" (Ephesians 2:19).

The church consists of people from every race and nationality who are brothers and sisters in Christ. Love, acceptance, and forgiveness are an essential part of family life. Although ultimately God is the Father of us all, there are also spiritual fathers and mothers within the church who help other family members grow into the fullness of God's calling for their lives.

4. The Church is Jesus' bride.

"'For this reason a man will leave his father and mother and be united to his wife, and the two will become one flesh.' This is a profound mystery—but I am talking about Christ and the church" (Ephesians 5:31-32 NIV).

The church is being prepared for the great day when Jesus returns and we are united forever. The metaphor of a bride celebrates our final union with Christ, the Head and Husband of the church. Worship is our expression of reverence, love, and close relationship with Him.

5. The Church is the Lord's army.
"A final word: Be strong in the Lord and in his mighty power. Put on all of God's armor so that you will be able to stand firm against all strategies of the devil" (Ephesians 6:10-11).

The Church is armed and equipped as soldiers, standing together against the powers and strategies of darkness. We are called to be victorious over the spiritual foes who oppose God's will and who attempt to work against us.

PLANTED IN THE HOUSE

A word picture that describes our connection to the local church is the idea of being "planted." We looked at Psalm 92:12 earlier. It says, "The righteous shall flourish like a palm tree, he shall grow like a cedar in Lebanon. Those who are planted in the house of the Lord shall flourish in the courts of our God" (NKJV).

To be a part of a local church means planting your life and establishing yourself with roots that go down in the life of the church. When you plant yourself in God's house, you will flourish and grow.

THINGS TO THINK ABOUT

1. Why is it important for people to understand God's design for the church?

2. What changes and results have you seen in your life from being planted in a church?

John's Story

I am from a country that used to be part of the Soviet Union. I was born into a Muslim family, and when I was young I followed God the best way I knew, which was by going to the mosque.

When I was about eleven years old, my parents divorced. At that time divorce in the family was a disgrace. Teachers and students started making fun of me in class. Before this I had been a very active child in school, but my family situation hit me so hard that I retreated into a shell. At night I would talk to the only God I knew about my feelings and tell him I didn't want to live. Sometimes I even considered ending my life, but at other times I would dream about the future and tell God I wanted to have the best possible family when I grew up, with a loving, caring wife and awesome kids.

When I grew a bit older, the Soviet Union fell apart. Our country was suffering economically, and my family was too. My father had passed away, and starting at a very young age, I was forced to work to help support the family.

One day I decided to go to the mosque because I remembered my childhood prayers and realized only God could help me. I started to do the Muslim prayers regularly, but there was a deep emptiness inside that wasn't satisfied.

My mother decided to sell our apartment and buy a house, as we were a big family of seven children and needed more space. Unfortunately, we were swindled and lost most of our money, and we ended up in a small, one-bedroom apartment. The good thing, however, was that my future wife lived in this apartment building, and we had the opportunity to meet! Her name was Naomi.

One day I talked to Naomi about going to the mosque, and she invited me to church with her. I told her she was part of a cult and I didn't want to hear any more about this, even though by this time we had become good friends.

In our country men considered themselves on a higher level than women and would never open up and share their hearts with a girl. But for some reason, I trusted Naomi and told her everything that was on my heart. We became close friends, but I never considered marrying her.

But the time came that my younger brother wanted to get married. In our culture, the older brother was required to marry first. So my younger brother started putting pressure on me to marry so he could get married. I asked Naomi if she had any girlfriends she could introduce me to. She introduced me to a few of her friends, but I wasn't especially interested in any of them.

Then, one New Year, my friend told me he wanted to get married and asked me to hook him up with Naomi. In our culture at the time, many people practiced "bride kidnapping." A young man would "kidnap" a woman and propose to her, and although she could refuse, in most cases she had little option but to marry the man. So in essence my friend was asking me to help him kidnap my good friend Naomi so she could become his bride.

We made the plan, and I got her in the car, but on the way to this friend's house, I started to reconsider. Naomi was my good friend, and I wanted her to have the best future possible; and I realized this guy wasn't the person for her. So we turned the car around and drove off, and that day I saved her from marrying my friend!

About a year later, I decided to marry her myself, and we started a serious relationship. However, I began to get involved in drugs, crime, and other bad habits. I was arrested and given a three-and-a-half year prison sentence. I started praying to whoever God was. I didn't know if He was Allah or Buddha or whoever. I asked Him to get me out of prison. After four months, I was miraculously released.

More than ever, I wanted to get married to Naomi as soon as possible. But she was now unsure, as she was getting advice from her pastor and leaders not to marry this "Muslim criminal." But she kept praying for me, and she felt like God was leading her in the relationship and He would do great things in my life.

One day, according to our custom, I kidnapped her. I tricked her and told her we were going to a birthday party at my friend's house, but when I got her in the car, I took her to my brother's house instead. There I declared she would be my bride. Her parents came and tried to take her back home, but she agreed to stay and be my wife.

My younger brother married shortly after me, and after three months his wife became pregnant and within a year had a baby. However, my wife could not become pregnant, and in our culture this was a real disgrace for a man. Conflict started in our home as I blamed my wife for not being able to have a child.

My family had a very bad reputation. There were always scandals going on around us. We often got drunk, fought, and beat each other up. All of our relatives disowned us, saying, "We don't want our children associating with this family." One of my brothers was a drug dealer; another was an alcoholic.

My wife was like an angel in our family. I started to feel sorry for her. She always did the right thing. She didn't drink or party with us, and she was always kind and humble.

I decided to divorce her because I felt sorry for her. I felt I didn't deserve her as a wife. I kept trying to create reasons why we should divorce. I would come home drunk and beat her.

One day I gambled a lot of money away and came home very late with stains on my good suit. I threw the dirty suit in the corner and went to bed, thinking when I got up and the suit was still dirty, I would blame her and ask for a divorce. I got up early looking for the suit and found it clean and pressed, hanging in the closet.

That night, I started talking to God again, and He touched me. I said, "I don't know who you are—if you are Allah or Buddha or Jesus—but help me!" I remembered when I was a child and prayed *about having a good family. "God, I want a good, loving family, but I need to change. Please help me!"*

I didn't know it at the time, but my wife was in the other room listening to my prayer. She was praying too! That was the beginning of my walk with God. I committed my life to Him all by myself, not in a church.

I knew my wife kept a notebook where she wrote down the things she learned in church. I was too proud to ask to read it, so I stole it from her. As I didn't know much yet, I would turn toward Mecca and read the words in the book. I didn't realize they were words from songs they sang in church!

Not long after that, I was invited to a Christmas service at a church. The meeting hall was filled with children. They were singing, and they looked so happy. At the end of the service, I went forward and publicly acknowledged Jesus as my Savior. A few days later, I went to a water baptism class at the church. When I arrived home, my wife was crying. I asked, "Why are your crying?"

She said, "I'm pregnant!"

We had a daughter, and we named her "Mercy," because we knew God's mercy had come to us.

I started to serve in the church right away, telling all my friends that the Bible was truth. They thought I had gone crazy. My whole family turned against me, but now my wife and I were on the same side. Every Saturday there was a big scandal with my family warning us not to go to church and threatening us. But we always found a reason to sneak away and go to church.

My wife and I started to pray for my family. We would stay up late at night and pray. We didn't even know how to pray, but we quoted Scripture and we pleaded with God for the salvation of my family. Several times, late at night, I walked ten kilometers to my mother's home, placed my hands on the outside of the house, prayed for Jesus to enter the home, then walked home again.

One of my brothers had served in the army and had come back very disturbed. He was the one who became an alcoholic. His wife left him, and his family was ruined. One day he called me and said he wanted to talk because he had seen a change in my life. He had tried to talk to our other brothers and sisters about his problems, but no one would listen to him. I was the only one who cared.

I listened for a long time and finally had the courage to ask if I could pray for him. God immediately delivered him from alcohol, drugs, and everything else. Today he runs a rehab center where he helps others find God and deliverance.

When my family saw the change in my brother, several of my brothers and sisters started to believe. We kept praying for my mother. When I was young, I hated my mother so much for the pain her divorce caused me that I wanted to kill her. But God had changed my heart and given me a deep love for her. One day she asked to talk to me. She said, "I've noticed you've changed. You've become a better person, not drinking and fighting anymore. Your wife also is not so bad, but I still don't like her."

By this time my mother had become quite successful. She had a nice home and a small restaurant that she owned. She said to me that day, "I will give you the home and the business. All you need to do is stop going to church." She was embarrassed before her friends that her family was Christian and going to church.

Of course I wanted to have a nice home, job, and money. But I said, "I would rather be one of your workers and keep going to church than be the owner and have lots of privileges." I told her that if I stopped going to church, I would most likely go back to my old ways. My mother didn't say anything, but I believe this deeply impacted her.

By this time I had been invited several times to share my testimony at church in my native language. When I got saved, there were only a few local children in the church (who mostly came for the presents that were given out) and the older Korean ladies who had started the church. However, through my testimony and ministry, many people from my ethnic people group got saved and started to come to church.

One Sunday, I was invited to preach for the first time. I spent hours preparing. I dressed in my best clothes and went to church. I was standing at the front speaking when I saw my mother enter the church! I thought, "Oh no, she's come to cause a scandal!" She came in and sat at *the very back with one of my brothers.*

I quickly changed my message and began to talk about salvation: how Jesus had come and given His life for us. Then I gave the invitation, and four people came forward, including my mother! I prayed the sinner's prayer, and they repeated it after me. I was crying, my mother was crying, and even the others who had come forward were crying. Later I found out the other three didn't know she was my mother, and they cried because they saw us crying and thought that's what they were supposed to do when they prayed the sinner's prayer.

On the day of my mother's baptism, she went into the water in a lot of pain. She was paralyzed on one side as the result of a stroke years before. She came out of the water totally healed!

A week later, she was invited to share her story on our local television channel. All our relatives who were convinced our family was cursed now call us blessed. Whenever they have a problem in their families, they call my mother to pray for them. Today my mother leads the prayer ministry in our church.

I have four children and the wonderful family I always dreamed of. Of course there have been difficult times. In 2005 the government took away our church registration, and things became difficult for us. We had grown to about seventy people, and one day the authorities came and arrested us all. Our pastor left for another city.

Every time I was arrested, I would share with the authorities how Jesus had changed my life. But I was still fined, and sometimes I had to spend days and weeks in jail. The church was forced to meet secretly in home groups. Because of the persecution and fear, people gradually stopped meeting, until there were only about five people left: my mother, a few relatives, and me. We were forced to start the church all over again.

Gradually, as we prayed and shared about Jesus, people started to come to Christ. Today we meet secretly in small groups of two or three, but we are reaching over one hundred people.

The hardest test for me was when my assistant was arrested and sentenced to seven years in prison. We knew if he was sent to the prison for hardened criminals, he would be killed. We prayed and prayed, and

God gave us faith he would be released.

The judge was changed the day before his final trial, and a woman was put in place. She studied the case and said, "I can't find any reason for this man to be in prison," and she released him!

Every time we are called in for questioning or accused of some crime, I testify to the judges and authorities about what God has done in my life. Then I ask, "Do you want me to turn away from the God who has changed me and done all these miracles in my life?"

They always shake their heads and say, "No, we don't want you to turn away from your God. This is just our job. This is what we are required to do."

A few years ago, I felt very alone. Our founding pastor had left, and we were no longer in touch with each other. I was without a pastor. I was searching for someone I could be accountable to. During that time, I met a friend named Victoria who told me about Home Church.

God had given my team and me a vision of a hub with spokes, and we knew we were to launch many church locations in our area. When Victoria shared with me that God had given the same vision to the founders of Home Church many years earlier, I knew we should become part of the Home Church family. Pastor Mel is now my pastor and friend, and we feel so blessed to be part of this family.

VALUES
*Who you are and
why you do what you do*

DAY 11

Values Shape the Future
Values shape the church and set the future.

ON THE THIRTY-FIFTH anniversary of Home Church, I remember standing in front of our congregation of several hundred people and thinking a rather strange thought: "I really love these people, but I no longer love this church. This isn't the church I want to pastor as we look toward the future. It's time for change."

The church I had led for the last few decades had become a wonderful, well-respected church with six different locations around Alberta. But like many churches, we had lost our edge, we had lost our way, and we needed to find it again.

We had become a church for a generation from the past, and we desperately needed an upgrade if we were to reach present and future generations. The problem was that I didn't know what changes needed to be made or how to make them. We needed to know God's will for our future.

Dissatisfaction is often a tool to bring about change. This is different than discontent, which is a result of unbelief and ungratefulness. Dissatisfaction or discomfort with our current situation usually motivates us to grow, improve, and find solutions.

I called a good friend of mine, Steve Murrell, and told him my dilemma over the telephone. "Steve, I love the people, but I don't like the way we are doing church. Can you give me some advice?"

Steve is an amazing leader, and I highly respect his opinion and experience. He oversees the "Every Nation" movement and is the founder of a great church in the Philippines which has eighty thousand people in weekly attendance in multiple services around the Manila metropolitan area. It is a world-reaching church that models what practical discipleship is all about.

Steve answered my question by sharing a concept that would change our church forever. "Mel, you must reshape the values of the church. When you do, you will set the future. Your values will lead you on your way to a great future."

I responded, "Will you come to Red Deer and help us? Would you be willing to help our church team and network of leaders rediscover who we are and reset the values of the church?"

Steve graciously agreed to come, and we set a date. We invited about fifty leaders to the meeting, some seated around a large table and the rest in a circle around the room. For two hours we discussed our history and beliefs. We described in detail who we are, what we had accomplished, and what was most important to us.

Steve instructed us to summarize our identity and calling as a church and write our conclusions on large posters which we posted around the room. Here are just a few of the things that identified us:

1. A Bible-believing church
2. A Spirit-empowered church
3. A disciple-making church
4. A missions-sending church
5. A faith-based church
6. A church that believes in the power of prayer
7. A church that develops leaders
8. A church that believes in the five-fold ministry gifts of Ephesians 4
9. A multi-site church
10. A church that believes in miracles
11. A church that believes people should prosper
12. A church with a strong biblical foundation

13. A practical church that teaches people how to live
14. A church that values and practices relationship
15. A church that gathers weekly as a congregation and in small groups

We completed reviewing our history and beliefs around three o'clock in the afternoon. Then Steve said, "Now we are going to take the things we've written down and funnel them into five major values. These values will be the foundations on which your culture will be established. They will clearly identify who you are and what you are called to do. They will reshape the church, help you reach your community and make disciples, and establish your future."

I vividly remember leading this pivotal discussion. We began to write value statements on a large board, and at the end of the day, we had agreed on five major statements that are now the core values of Home Church. These values, which I will describe in more detail in the following chapters, are:

1. Engage the Culture
2. Live in Authentic Relationships
3. Empower the Potential of People
4. Driven by Compassion
5. For All Generations

As a church, we know who we are, what we are called to do, and what is important to us. We are not always seeking new direction because we have a clear mandate from the Holy Spirit. The future has been set for years to come.

VALUES RE-EVALUATED

Values are the path the church travels on. They determine who you are and what you are called to do. They shape the future.

Values can and should be re-evaluated periodically. Make sure your values reflect who you want to be, not just who you have been. The future does not have to be determined by the same values that originally set the church in motion. We live in a changing world, and in order to lead, the church must be willing to change. The message of good news is the same, but the presentation must take on new forms in order to reach present and future generations.

Before that meeting with Steve, we had been a church focused on the Bible, prayer, worship, and the gifts of the Spirit. There is nothing wrong with that—those are still foundational beliefs for us—but we realized our focus had turned inward. Even though we had started on the streets of Red Deer as a church for the city, over time we had become a church for the churched. We existed for ourselves more than for others.

When we recognized our calling to engage the world with the message of Jesus, we began to make very practical changes. We changed our procedure for receiving tithes and offerings, for example. We also stopped singing certain songs. Our rule of thumb became this: if a first-time guest couldn't understand the lyrics, we changed the song. We started singing more about Jesus: who He is, what He can do, and how much He loves us.

Once we determined our core values, things began to change in our church. It was a process that occurred over several years, but the long-term fruit is obvious to us all now. Home Church is focused on people, on relationships, on the city, and on reaching the world.

A church that redevelops its values can reshape its culture and set the future for coming years. Like a caterpillar that spins a cocoon and then begins to stir, struggle, and stretch, so the church must break out of its former identity to become the church of the future.

THINGS TO THINK ABOUT

1. What values do you need to change that are limiting your growth and impact?

2. Can you identify the values of your church?

3. How are you living out the values and mission of your church?

Engage the Culture
*Engaging our culture is the key to
changing our culture.*

WHEN WE ARRIVED in Red Deer in 1972, our group of believers engaged the culture continuously. It was one of our core values. We were always on the streets of Red Deer, connecting with people and sharing the good news of Jesus with everyone we could.

I remember one time, however, when I missed a key opportunity to engage the culture. Our group of new believers was making headlines in the newspaper and becoming known in the community, and I received an invitation from a city official to sit with a panel of leaders to discuss the needs of the troubled youth of the city. I turned down the invitation because I thought I was too busy preaching the gospel to take time out for this group. This was a huge mistake and a missed opportunity to engage with key people of influence.

As Christians we must be careful not to miss the opportunities that come our way to engage culture. We can get so focused on church-related opportunities that we miss the open doors to impact the very culture we are called to reach. Every person in the church is commissioned by God to engage their neighbors, friends, business associates, and others with the goal of showing God's love, sharing their own experience with Christ, and telling the good news of Jesus.

SALT AND LIGHT

Engaging the culture is the key to changing the culture. Engaging the community should be the intentional action of every follower of Jesus. We need people in all sectors of society who can be salt, light, and leaven and bring change to their communities (Matthew 5:13-16; 13:33). We are the "salt of the earth" and the "light of the world."

Jesus came to earth as a man, lived among us, and engaged our culture in every way possible, yet without sin. He didn't shy away or remain aloof from the problems and sin of humanity, but He came and lived among us. In the same way, we are called to be *in* the world but not *of* the world, and we are meant to change the world around us. The church must relate in a relevant way to the culture it is in and bring the message of good news so everyone can be saved.

To engage the culture means to do everything within our reach to influence and reach the society in which we are called to minister. Different tools are required to reach different cultures, generations, and social contexts. We must be creative and willing to adapt our presentation to reach as many people as possible.

The apostle Paul believed in engaging the community creatively. He said, "I try to find common ground with everyone, doing everything I can to save some. I do everything to spread the Good News and share in its blessings" (1 Corinthians 9:22-23).

FIND A NEED AND FILL IT

Our church is in many different nations and cultures, and not all of them are friendly to the church or the good news of Jesus. Clearly there have to be different approaches and tools to engage different cultures.

We have found that to engage and reach a culture, you first find a need and fill it. What does the community and culture around you lack? How can you supply the need? If we are faithful to love and serve people, God will open doors to share the good news with them.

In Rwanda, Africa, we engaged the culture by feeding hungry children. Often we would first approach the mayors of particular towns we wanted to help. We would say, "We'd like to come to your community and feed the hungry children. Will you donate one franc for every four francs we provide?" The mayors would usually agree and invite us into their communities. As we gave food to many families, we also shared the good news of Jesus with them. The mayors would see our genuine love and generosity, and they would end up endorsing our efforts. On some occasions, they even provided land where we could establish church buildings. We were able to plant strong churches in a short amount of time because we met the immediate, practical needs of people in the name of Jesus and with the love of Jesus.

IT'S ABOUT PEOPLE

Engaging culture isn't difficult. It simply means connecting with people and building authentic relationships outside of the church. As we show God's love and grace beyond the walls of the church, barriers and resistance to the message are removed, and people who might never have come to church are able to receive the good news in their homes, neighborhoods, and workplaces.

A few years ago in Home Church, we began using summer "block parties" to connect with people who would not normally come to church. Every home in a section of the city receives an invitation to a fun, outdoor party. We organize crafts for the kids and serve hot dogs, hamburgers, and many flavors of snow cones. These events allow us to meet neighbors, form friendships, talk about Jesus, and invite people to church, all in an authentic, organic way.

These block parties are a big part of our summer now. From June through September, we host thousands of people and see hundreds of decisions to follow Jesus. Many churches stop evangelism during the summer, but we have found it is a great opportunity to build friendships and engage culture.

THINGS TO THINK ABOUT

1. Where has God called you to be the light and the salt of the earth?

2. What needs do you see in your community?

3. What creative things could you do to engage the community where God has placed you?

Rick's Story

My upbringing was not great. My mother and father split up when I was five years old. I have a few happy memories from before their separation. I remember my father coming home from the oil patch and our border collie, Skippy, always running at him and jumping on his chest, sometimes knocking him to the ground. My siblings and I—all seven of us—were always so excited whenever he would come home. After my father left for the last time, I remember continually asking my mother, "When is my daddy going to come home?"

My parents' divorce left a huge hole in my heart, a hole filled with anger, sorrow, and rebellion. That anger would only grow as the years went on.

My mother had a hard time raising all of us on her own. When I was seven years old, she met a man, and we moved in with him and lived on his farm. We were excited at first, but it was short-lived because the man would drink heavily and beat my mother and us kids.

Our neighbors had a couple of boys the same age as my younger brother and me. These boys introduced us to alcohol when I was still just seven years old. I drank steadily from then until I was thirty-six. Cigarettes and drugs came into the picture shortly thereafter, when I was about ten.

By the time I was twelve, things had gone from bad to worse. I got into a lot of fights at school and was often in the principal's office. My mother's boyfriend would constantly drink and beat us. I could not get away from my mother's screams. I would hide in the basement closet and plug my ears when they would fight, but I could still hear her shrieks of terror. I wanted to kill that man for all the pain he was causing our family.

Several times I ran away from home and lived on the streets, hanging out and partying with others who were in similar circumstances. I was only twelve, but I learned street smarts quickly to survive. Eventually the police would pick me up and take me home; but it wouldn't be long before I was back on the streets of another town or city.

Soon I realized I could make money selling drugs. This became a big part of my life. I was both a user and a dealer. Many of those days are just a blur because I constantly mixed drugs and alcohol. It didn't matter what drug or what kind of alcohol—I did them all.

When I was about fifteen, I played football in school. One day I looked in the mirror and realized my muscles had developed quite a bit. I swore to myself that if that man ever touched my mother again, he was going to get what was coming to him.

Soon enough, it happened. I was downstairs in my room. I knew they were drinking, and I could hear them arguing. I heard a slap and then a thud as my mother hit the floor. I ran upstairs as fast as I could and jumped the guy. I bent him over a chair and started choking him and punching him in the face over and over with all my strength. I screamed at him, "I am way stronger than you! You are never going to touch anyone in my family again!"

I don't think I would have quit punching him, but my mother started screaming frantically, "Stop! Stop! You're going to kill him!"

I stopped. His limp body was dangling over the chair, and there was blood everywhere. If I remember correctly, we dragged him out of the back door and called the police.

Enough was enough. I ran away again, but this time I went far away—about a thousand miles away. I kept selling drugs, I worked different jobs, and I spent a lot of time fighting and hanging out with the wrong people. About a year later I returned home. I discovered my oldest brother was in jail. He had also had enough of that man beating my mother, and one day he broke the man's jaw and almost killed him.

Amazingly the school in my town allowed me to go back to class, and somehow I graduated. In the coming years, I got married, and we had two kids. I started a couple of businesses. But the patterns of addiction and dysfunction I had learned since childhood continued. My marriage eventually fell apart when I caught my wife with another man. That brought me to the end of myself. All my heart's desires were wrapped up in having a family and a loving wife, and I felt like a failure.

Over the next few years, something strange happened. Person after person kept telling me about this guy named Jesus. Honestly I was not too interested. One man gave me a Bible and told me to read Proverbs. I came across a verse that says, "It's better to live alone in the corner of an attic than with a quarrelsome wife in a lovely home." I almost did a back flip—this was unbelievable! How did this guy Jesus know exactly what I had been going through?

One gentlemen in particular kept inviting me to church. One day he said something I hadn't heard before: "There are some very pretty girls at our church."

That was all I needed to hear. "Let's go!"

Once I entered the church, I sat in the back, just gazing around. People were very friendly. This pastor named Mel Mullen started preaching. I couldn't believe what I was hearing—it seemed like he was standing right in front of me, and everything he said stabbed me straight in the heart. It was amazing. At the end of the service, he invited people forward to give their lives to God. It felt like something invisible was ushering me up to the front. I couldn't resist. On the way up there, I remember thinking, "Okay God, I know I need you in my life. Take me. I'm yours. But don't think I'm going to settle for mediocrity."

I floated out to the parking lot and drove away. No sooner did I hit the highway than I began hearing in my head, "No more drugs; no more alcohol; no more cigarettes," over and over. By the time I got home, I was crying out to God and thanking Him. I knew in my heart the bondage was over and I would never be without a Father again. That was June 8, 1995. Since that supernatural deliverance, I have not had any cigarettes, alcohol, or drugs.

Today I am married to a truly beautiful, inspiring, faithful woman, and God has put our families together. So far we have ten grandchildren. The Lord also allowed me to reconcile with my dad when I was thirty-six years old, after I shared my testimony with him. It was the first time my dad said, "I love you, Son." To God be all the glory!

Authentic Relationships
No one needs to be lonely.

OVER THE COURSE of my ministry, I have seen a number of well-known pastors experience moral failure. For the most part, they were sincere, good leaders; but somehow, they ended up making very poor choices.

I saw the damage their mistakes produced in their own lives, in the churches they led, and in the body of Christ as a whole, and it was a wake-up call for me. I realized how unwise it was to walk alone or work alone in the ministry. My wife and I realized for our own blessing and protection, we needed people who could speak into our lives; and our church needed the security and stability that comes from outside counsel.

Heather and I sat down with Mel Davis, a pastor from Vancouver, Canada, who was a spiritual father to us, and asked him, "Will you be our pastor?" It was an important moment to us. We realized the significance of what we were doing by voluntarily submitting ourselves to his leadership.

God never intended humans to live life alone. We were created for companionship, for relationship, for family. That holds true whether you are a pastor, leader, church member, or simply someone seeking to know more about God. We all need other people in our lives.

I remember my son, Jachin, saying to our church staff in 2016, "No one should be lonely." It's a simple but profound truth. He went on to stress how important it is to connect with people who attend church and to make sure everyone is receiving love, developing friends, and experiencing healthy and wholesome relationships.

As a church, we are committed to this principle. We even host annual conferences in several nations called "Friendships for Life." At these conferences, the churches that relate to us and each other within those countries or regions gather for training, fellowship, and encouragement. We have seen how important it is to take a few days each year to focus on these relationships. It helps produce safety, health, and wholeness for the people in the churches that are represented.

PURSUING AUTHENTIC RELATIONSHIPS

Relationships do not just happen. They are a choice, and they are the result of focused pursuit. Years ago, I decided to pursue relationships with key people I wanted to have as friends. Many of the great relationships I have now would not have happened if I had not initiated the relationship. When I began this pursuit, our church was very small; but I invited some of the speakers I admired from around the world to come to our church. We became friends, and today I have friends in many nations.

It's not enough to just have relationships: we must have *authentic* relationships. Relationships must be real, not religious. People don't want to attend a church where no one greets them or befriends them. They don't want to sit in church and look at the back of someone's head but never experience a relationship connection. We all want to connect with people on a real, practical, and genuine level.

God is a God of relationship. He values and invests in relationships, so much so that He sent Jesus to Earth to reestablish the relationship with Him that had been broken through sin.

Now, He expects His body, the church, to be a place of healthy, life-giving relationships with one other.

LAYERS OF RELATIONSHIP

God wants us to have well-connected, layered relationships with people. Ephesians 2:21 says, "Now He's using you, fitting you in brick by brick, stone by stone, with Christ Jesus as the cornerstone that holds all the parts together" (MSG).

Authentic relationships are like bricks or stones in a wall, or like the layers of scales on a crocodile: they are tightly layered and so perfectly fitted together that nothing can cause damage or separation. Here are a few suggestions to develop layered relationships with many people.

1. Layer your relationships in unity.
Disunity is never God's plan. When God finds relationships that are united, He sends His blessing (Psalm 133). When He sees people who are walking together in unity, He declares, "I am there among them" (Matthew 18:19). When He finds people who are united and who speak the same language—that is, who are unified in their goals, labor, and communication—He says, "nothing they set out to do will be impossible for them" (Genesis 11:5).

2. Layer your relationships in covenant.
A covenant relationship is based on more than feelings: it is a mutual decision to seek the good of one another and to not allow anything to bring division. The relationship between David and Jonathan is a profound picture of a covenant relationship built on love. After David killed Goliath, Jonathan and David became close friends. Jonathan even gave up his right to the throne because he knew his covenant friend David was called

by God to be king instead of him. Their bond of friendship and commitment lasted a lifetime.

3. Layer your relationships in the love of God.
Relationships inevitably face moments of disagreement, misunderstanding, or offense—but true love enables our relationships to outlast even the most difficult times. Peter wrote, "Most important of all, continue to show deep love for each other, for love covers a multitude of sins" (1 Peter 4:8). God's love is the greatest love, and He enables us to love one another as He loves us. As we follow Jesus, we will naturally love others with God's unconditional, authentic love.

4. Layer your relationships in trust.
Trust means we give each other the benefit of the doubt. It means we choose to believe the best about someone even when there might be opportunity to take up an offense. Paul described true love this way: "Love never gives up, never loses faith, is always hopeful, and endures through every circumstance" (1 Corinthians 13:7).

Relationships aren't always easy, but they are well worth the effort. They are a gift from God, and they are one of the most important resources we have. As we learn to pursue healthy, authentic relationships and layer them in unity, covenant, love, and trust, our lives will become more stable and secure than ever before.

THINGS TO THINK ABOUT

1. Do you have friends that can speak into your life?

2. What benefits have you experienced from the relationships in your life?

3. Are your relationships layered in unity, covenant, the love of God, and trust? Specifically, who do you have this level of relationship with?

DAY 14

Empower Potential
Help people become who they're destined to be.

WHEN MY CHILDREN, Jachin and Christy, were growing up, they used to sing, "I am a bundle of potentiality." I will never forget their sweet voices as they tried to pronounce "potentiality."

They probably didn't know exactly what they were singing at the time, but as they grew up, we worked hard to instill confidence in them that they could reach their potential. We believed they had a great future, and it was our responsibility as parents to help develop their potential.

It's relatively easy to believe in children's potential because they have their whole lives in front of them. But it is just as important to believe in the potential of every person we encounter—including ourselves—and do whatever we can to help people fulfill the calling on their lives. Every person is of immeasurable value and importance to God. We all have great potential in Him, and that potential must be developed and empowered.

CALLED TO EMPOWER

When I was a young pastor, I had to wrestle with the question, "Am I called to help people get to where they need to go in life?" I knew I was called to preach the gospel and train people in the teachings of God, but was I also called to empower them to reach their potential? Was our church meant to play a role in developing people in their calling and purpose?

I came to the conclusion that yes, I am called to help people develop their potential. My goal isn't to make them just "good Christians" or to get them to volunteer in the church. It is to help them become who they were meant to be and to accomplish what God called them to do.

Likewise the role of the church is to help people become who they are destined by God to be, both in the church and in their unique spheres of influence. Discipleship means making great followers of Jesus, establishing them in the principles of the Word of God, and training them to maximize their potential as individuals, in their families, in their businesses, and in their calling and purpose in the world.

When I realized I was not only called to preach the good news of Jesus and make disciples but to help people become who they are called to be and get to where they need to go in life, I began to see things differently. I discovered a passion within me to empower people. This change of mindset radically affected how I thought about people. It changed my relationships and my messages. My goal, and the goal of the church, became to maximize the potential of those around me in every way possible.

Empowering potential was the impetus behind Destiny Christian School. This is a K-9 school we established to develop our children and maximize every child's potential. Over the years we have had the privilege of investing in the lives of hundreds of children.

Empowering potential is why we started Success Builders, a movement of business leaders that helps business and professional people become all they are called to be. I began mentoring business leaders many years ago because I saw so many great leaders not maximizing their potential, and I wanted to do something about it. I believe it is God's plan for people to create wealth, both for their own well-being and for the kingdom of God. Today, Success Builders hosts regular training in many nations, empowering people to be successful.

Empowering potential is the reason many of our business leaders travel to other nations, investing time and money to help people get out of poverty and have opportunities to become successful. They often provide micro-loans to people in other nations who want to go into business for themselves as a practical way to help them take steps toward their dreams.

GOD SEES YOUR POTENTIAL

God sees greater potential in us than we see in ourselves. He said through the prophet Jeremiah, "I know the plans I have for you . . . They are plans for good and not for disaster, to give you a future and a hope" (Jeremiah 29:11). This message was given to people who had been scattered to the furthest parts of the Babylonian empire by King Nebuchadnezzar. God saw a future for people they did not see for themselves. He promised they would return to the land of Israel, their fortunes would be restored, and they would reach their potential.

In the Bible, when people met God, they discovered He had bigger plans for them than they had for themselves. When Gideon was threshing grain while hiding in a winepress, God called him a "mighty hero" (Judges 6:12). God knew Gideon would become the leader of Israel and deliver the people from the oppression of Midian.

Similarly, God saw in Moses a great leader. He didn't leave him in the wilderness, limited in his potential to just feeding a few sheep. He spoke to Moses out of a burning bush and sent him to Egypt to deliver Israel from bondage.

The Bible records the stories of great leaders, politicians, doctors, lawyers, builders, and business people. It is a book about careers, potential, plans, and futures. It is a book that gives us the promise of great success and the tools to achieve it (Joshua 1:8). It is a book of empowerment: it encourages and equips us to fulfill our purposes in life.

Salvation is not just a one-time experience with God where your sins are forgiven. It is a package: a whole-life transformation that includes your future. God knows what you can become both in the church and in the world around you. He has a plan for you and He knows your potential. He sees things in you that you do not even see in yourself.

THINGS TO THINK ABOUT

1. What do you think God has called you to accomplish or become in the future?

2. What steps can you take this week to move into your calling?

3. How can you help empower potential in the people around you?

Melanie's story

I came to Home Church in 1996. I was newly saved and incredibly broken. There wasn't any area of life that was untouched by pain. I had lost my child, my marriage, my home, my relationships, and my work. My heart felt broken beyond repair, void of hope or dreams. I was alive but not living, doing my best to just navigate each day.

Today, there is no sign of brokenness in me anywhere. I am healed and whole and have experienced incredible restoration in every area of life. The church made that possible.

The church provided the opportunity to continue the relationship with Christ I had already experienced, the opportunity to take personal responsibility for my life, and the opportunity to contribute what I had, no matter how insignificant it was.

When people met me for the first time, they could have heard my story and taken pity on me, telling me to take a seat on the sidelines while they took care of me and I got "better." Everyone could see how broken I was. They could hear my grief and my pain when I spoke. They could sense my failure. But they didn't tell me that. Instead they made room for me to belong and to give what I had. They empowered the potential in me by expecting me to contribute.

The first time someone invited me to be part of a prayer meeting, I was very surprised. I remember thinking to myself, "Really? You think I could pray?" I didn't think I had anything to give. It would have made more sense for them to pray for me! As time passed I was invited to participate in other ways, such as helping with the singles ministry or being a part of events that were happening. There were no titles or positions, just work that needed to be done along with smiles and invitations to be part of what was going on.

No one could change my circumstances, take away my pain, or heal my broken heart. But they gave me the greatest gift they had, a gift that would rebuild my life, by offering me a place to contribute. In giving what I had and being part of something bigger than myself, God healed my heart, set me on my feet, and began the process of making me whole.

If people had seen my brokenness and told me I had nothing to give, they would have crippled me for life. Instead they invited me to give what I had, and they watched the miracle of God rebuilding my life.

This is God's design. We see it in the story of the widow in 2 Kings 4 who goes to the prophet because she has lost everything and the creditors are coming to take her two sons. Not only is everything gone, but her future is also about to be lost.

The prophet's answer seems to be a contradiction. He asks, "How can I help you? What do you have in your house?" It seems like he is unsure whether he should help her or she should help herself. But the prophet knew the power of God works with what we have, no matter how insignificant, to create our future.

The widow told the prophet she only had a flask of oil. He instructed her to borrow as many containers from her friends and neighbors as she could and to begin to pour out the oil she had. She began pouring, and supernaturally, the oil didn't stop flowing until she had filled every container she had. Then he told her to sell the oil, pay off her creditors, and live off the rest.

It's an incredible picture of how even when all has been lost, if we will give what we have in the opportunity before us, God will use what we have and bring restoration in our lives. I love Home Church. I've been on staff for over twenty years. I love what I do and the team of people I get to serve with. Through every year and every season, I have continued to give what I have in each opportunity. As I have poured out what God has given me, He has done what only He could do both in and through me. That is the incredible power of the church!

DAY 15

Driven by Compassion
Compassion is the key to all ministry.

"DRIVEN BY COMPASSION" is more than a motto or a catchy phrase to me. When I think of compassion, it has a name and a face: *Robert.*

Robert was a street boy in India, living with little food or clothing. He was desperate, destitute, starving. He was found and brought to Bob and Kay Hoover's "Home of Hope," a ministry in India and other nations that serves children in need. Bob and Kay were evangelists in India for many years. They were friends of ours and frequent speakers at our church for decades.

Heather and I became Robert's sponsors. We supported him financially, we sent letters, we prayed for him, and we watched him grow up. He went on to graduate with a nursing degree. Today he is one of our finest church leaders in India. Compassion changed Robert's life, and now he is a catalyst to bring hope and change to many others.

Jesus was "moved with compassion" when He saw the leper, so He reached out and healed him (Mark 1:41). Likewise He was "moved with compassion" when He saw the multitude like sheep without a shepherd (Mark 6:34). He told the story of the good Samaritan who "felt compassion" on the man who had fallen into the ditch (Luke 10:33). The Samaritan's compassion motivated him to get off his donkey, go to the man in the ditch, treat his wounds, carry him to a place where he could recover, and pay for his expenses.

Compassion is love in action. When our church adopted the value "Driven by Compassion," doors began to open in many nations to serve people in need. The call to raise up church locations that were engaged in feeding the poor, taking people from poverty, and helping them become self-sufficient and live in abundance became a mandate of Home Church.

Our church has always been a great church, but as we helped others, it became an even greater church. A Scripture that is the foundation of everything we do is 1 Samuel 3:8. "He lifts the poor from the dust and the needy from the garbage dump. He sets them among princes, placing them in seats of honor. For all the earth is the Lord's, and he has set the world in order."

Years after we began sponsoring Robert, our connection to Home of Hope grew even closer. After Bob passed away, Kay ran the ministry by herself, but eventually it came time to turn it over to someone else. She approached our church and asked us if we would assume responsibility for Hope of Home India. Our leadership team and church board accepted, and we began to oversee this amazing ministry in the middle of a poverty-stricken neighborhood in India. Today, Hope of Home sponsors nearly one thousand orphans in the Congo, India, Kenya, and Rwanda. We also help feed almost ten thousand children a month in these nations.

During my first trip to Africa, we visited Jabana, Rwanda, to attend the dedication of our first church there. I was with an amazing leader and pastor named Brian Thomson, who has worked on our team for nearly forty years. He oversees our Home Church ministry in Africa. (The incredible story about how God is using Brian to minister to children in need follows this chapter.)

At the dedication in Jabana, one of the leaders stood up and shared her story. She had lost her husband in the horrific Rwandan genocide. She and her children were homeless and living in extreme poverty. Then, as this heroic woman put it, "God sent Brian Thomson." Through partnership with Canadian sponsors, her life was put back together. She brought other homeless children into her home and raised them as well. Today her beautiful children are grown up and walking out God's plan in their lives.

On another occasion, our "One in a Million" women's conference raised $40,000 to take women from the worst of conditions in Africa and provide them a place to live, a micro loan to go into business, and an opportunity to live a better life.

"Driven by Compassion" is not only a value that affects the work we are doing as a church in India and Africa, but it's a motivation to help hurting people in all parts of the world, including close to home. In Canada all our church locations are engaged in local community projects as well as missions endeavors.

When one of our staff members, Barb Carritt, discovered that children coming on the bus did not have lunches due to financial hardship, she immediately took action. She began making bundles of five lunches every week for every child. Other people got involved, and today ten thousand lunches are given out yearly. The children are also given backpacks when school starts in the fall.

As another example of compassion, we have an annual drive called "Christmas Is for Everyone." We find families in need and take them turkey and everything they need for Christmas dinner, as well as toys for every child in the family.

If you would like to know more about Home of Hope and our compassion ministries, you can find more information on our website, *www.homeofhope.ca.*

The good news of Jesus means people do not have to remain enslaved by poverty or adverse circumstances. God wants to give them abundant life, both now and in heaven.

How does He bring people into this abundant life? Often, He uses other people, people who are driven by compassion to help those in need. Acts of compassion move people toward a relationship with God. Jesus was moved by compassion, and His church must be too. As we allow His compassion to lead us, we will bring hope and life to a hurting world.

THINGS TO THINK ABOUT

1. How would you define compassion?

2. What are some practical ways you can show compassion in your community?

Brian's Story
My Call to Feed the Children

I loved growing up on a farm west of Olds, Alberta, Canada. I always believed in God, but it wasn't until I was sixteen that Jesus became real to me and I became a Christian. I had always thought I would be a farmer, but I felt God speak to me for the first time in my life, and He showed me I was called to tell people all over the world about Jesus. A friend told me I should go to Bible college, so I did.

While I was attending Bible college, the teen Sunday school class in Olds needed a teacher, and I was asked to help. The Sunday class grew, and I also became the youth leader on Friday nights. At age twenty I took a job as a bus driver, I got married to Connie, and I started leading five youth groups in five small towns. Then Pastor Mel asked if I could help the youth ministry in Red Deer. God started pouring out His Holy Spirit, and many teenagers got saved. That was over thirty-two years ago!

Over time, Connie and I became involved in various areas of ministry, including starting a Bible college that Connie still leads today. I became the associate pastor and served God by leading worship, preaching often, and leading many departments of the church. Eventually I started to travel as a local church evangelist all across Canada, speaking in more than sixty different denominations and taking many mission trips around the world.

Then something happened that changed my life forever. In April 2006 God spoke to me clearly that I was to plant churches in Africa, to help rescue children there, and to take teams of people to help with compassion projects. I went to Rwanda in December for several days of preaching and ministry. I asked the pastor hosting me if he knew of any desperate children I could meet. He looked at me like I was crazy, because he was surrounded by them.

He took me to the "home" of a family who had nothing. The father had just died of AIDS two weeks before. The mother was in the hospital with AIDS, and the doctor had said she would die any day. I looked into the dark mud hut and saw four children with such sad eyes, all huddled together. They had no hope. I immediately felt my heart break, and I committed to sponsor them.

I went to the hospital with the pastor, and we prayed for their mom. Miraculously, she improved and was released from the hospital. She helped support her family for another nine years. At that time I didn't have a vision to help a lot of children, but I just did what I could do. We started sponsoring those four children, and I took pictures of twenty other desperate kids I met.

On the airplane home, someone sitting beside me asked me what I had been doing in Rwanda. I started talking, and immediately I began to cry. I hadn't cried once seeing the desperate children, but on the way home, I cried most of the way. I felt like God was filling my heart with His love. Romans 5:5 says, "he has given us the Holy Spirit to fill our hearts with his love."

When I arrived home, people asked me how my trip went. Again and again I would start crying as I told them about the children I had seen. People asked if they could join me and sponsor more children. When I spoke in the churches I was invited to, I couldn't help but talk about my life-changing experience, and more people and churches expressed their desire to get involved with monthly sponsorship.

We started helping twenty children, then fifty, then one hundred. God showed me Proverbs 28:27, which says, "Whoever gives to the poor will lack nothing." I felt like God was saying, "Take care of the poor, and I will take care of you."

One day, after we were sponsoring about five hundred children, I was praying and asked the Lord, "What do you want me to do to help children?" I felt an immediate reply that stunned me: "Help ten thousand children!" I didn't want to hear that, because it meant so much hard work and administration! But eventually I said yes to the Lord.

On another trip to Africa, while sharing the gospel at an outdoor evangelistic rally, I noticed hundreds of children with patches of hair missing due to malnutrition and toenails eaten away by disease from lack of shoes. I saw children scooping up yellowish-brown water from the ditches into water bottles to drink. I felt the Lord say to me, "If you walk on by these people and do nothing, the love of God is not in your heart." I was convicted by 1 John 3:17, "If someone has enough money to live well and sees a brother or sister in need but shows no compassion—how can God's love be in that person?"

I was helping as many children as I could with monthly sponsorships. I remember praying, "Jesus, please show me how I can help more children."

I felt the Lord speak to me from Mark 6:37. "You feed them."

I met with some of our African pastors, and we came up with a plan. I said, "Pastors, if you can raise money from local sponsors to feed twenty of the most desperate children a hot meal once a week, for one dollar a plate, I will try to find sponsors who can feed eighty children." I encouraged the pastors to make a list of the one hundred most desperate children within walking distance. Not just church kids, either—any kids in need.

It worked! Not only did they find local people who would donate small amounts of money, rice, and vegetables, but the local donors came to see what was happening and started getting saved. It was an "evangelistic feeding program." The children would learn about Jesus and get saved along with receiving a hot meal, and adults who came would also get saved and join the church. This is exactly what Matthew 5:16 teaches: "Let your light so shine before men, that they may see your good works and glorify your Father in heaven" (NKJV).

Our feeding and other social outreach ministries are collectively called Home of Hope. Since 2007 we have helped over ten thousand children in many different ways: rescuing babies thrown away in the garbage dumps of Nairobi, supporting children with monthly sponsorships, helping mothers become self-sustaining with micro-loans, providing animals to raise for food and other provisions, starting Christian schools, and feeding hot meals to over five thousand children a week through our feeding programs.

Besides the Home of Hope ministry, God has allowed us to start over one hundred churches in fifteen nations in Africa. One of our goals is to plant more churches in some of the most desperate areas of the continent. Each church will help one hundred of the neediest children in the area. We continue to train people in leadership and empower them to do what God has called them to do, and our team continues to grow. The best is yet to come!

Do you want to get involved? Would you like to help? For more information, visit www.homeofhope.ca.

DAY 16

For all Generations
Live for the generations to come.

NOT TOO LONG ago, Heather and I were able to connect with several distinct generations of family and friends within the space of a few weeks. It was an eye-opening experience to see the similarities and differences between them all.

First we visited the generation of our parents. We took a trip to the West Coast, where we saw a number of relatives who are in their eighties and nineties. We love this generation! In Canada, they brought the nation through the Great Depression of the thirties, and they laid a foundation for our prosperity today.

Next we visited some great friends of our generation. I love my generation too! We experienced the Holy Spirit bringing great renewal to the church at large, megachurches being born, and the good news of Jesus taking on new dimensions. We discovered (or rediscovered) so much about faith, prayer, church growth, and leadership.

After that we went camping with several friends of our daughter, Christy. This is the generation of our children, the new generation that has emerged to give leadership to the present-day church. What was most interesting was that even though we had a great time with our parents' generation and our own generation, it was our time with our children's generation that we enjoyed the most.

After our children, yet another generation is already beginning to arise. This is our grandchildren's generation. Even at their young age, they are already involved in leading in the church, and their greatest days are ahead.

As I think back over those memorable weeks and the four generations we encountered—parents, peers, children, and grandchildren—I realized once again that God is always looking toward the next generation. He extends His love and forgiveness to generation after generation without end. Exodus 20:6 says, "But I lavish unfailing love for a thousand generations on those who love Me and obey My commands."

The fact that God is looking toward the next generation doesn't mean He ignores older generations. God is a multi-generational God. He is the God of Abraham, Isaac, and Jacob (Exodus 3:6). Every age is important, and every generation needs every other generation.

I believe the church should value all generations but be especially focused on the *next* generation. A multi-generational church provides a place for everyone. It is the greatest church, because a multi-generational church always has its best days still ahead.

God's focus is always on the future, not the past. In His dealings with Israel, regardless of what had happened in the past, He gave promise after promise about the future. Jeremiah wrote, "'For I know the plans I have for you,' says the Lord. 'They are plans for good and not for disaster, to give you a future and a hope'" (Jeremiah 29:11).

When our grandkids were toddlers, our daughter-in-law, Becca, called us on more than one occasion and said, "Mom, we have an unexpected appointment. Could you take the boys for a couple of hours?" No matter what our evening plans were—maybe a dinner or movie date—Heather would cancel them. I wasn't even consulted. I didn't mind, though, because we were committed to our grandchildren.

It is obvious to most grandparents they should focus on the young generation. Grandchildren are a delight, and it is our joy to serve them. But too many times, churches don't have the same perspective toward young people. Only one or two generations are represented, and there is no place for younger people to step into leadership roles.

Churches and Jesus followers need to be committed to the generations to come. We need to choose to live our lives focused on the future. That means making whatever lifestyle changes are necessary to best serve the next generation. The older generation has to adapt to the younger. It must change more than the younger generation does in its style, worship, leadership structure, culture, dress, and more.

Becoming a future-focused follower of Jesus is so important. Unfortunately, many people get stuck in the past. They spend all their time remembering the "good old days" and focusing on what is behind them rather than the bright future before them. Their age is not the issue: their mindset is. They think old, act old, and respond old.

A proper understanding of the past is very important; however, the past cannot be the guiding power that directs our future. The past should be honored, but the focus of life must be on the future. Our future is hopeful and full of promise, and our lives should be lived for the generations to come. Brian Houston, senior pastor of Hillsong Church, says this: "Honor the past, live for today, build for the future." The *past* was good and the *present* is important, but the *future* is and always will be what we are building toward.

At our thirty-fifth anniversary, when I stood before the church and realized I didn't like the kind of church I was pastoring, a big part of it was the age demographic I observed. There were few young people or young families, and the vast majority of the church was over the age of thirty-five. I had to make a decision, and I did. I told my team, "We are going to focus young. We are going to train young people, we are going to give them tools to build the church for the next generation, and we are going to put leadership in their hands."

Now, years later, we are enjoying the fruit of those changes. A generation with more ability, better tools, and greater energy is leading the church into the future. Soon the time will come for them to transition leadership to their own children, and I am confident God will lead them in that process. The strength, creativity, and vitality of the younger generation coupled with the wisdom and experience of the older generation creates a healthy church culture.

As Christians we do not live our lives for ourselves, nor do we live in the past. We are people of the future who believe "the best is yet to come" as we move from generation to generation, from glory to glory.

THINGS TO THINK ABOUT

1. How can you close the generation gap by relating to and trusting people in a different stage of life?

2. How can you invest in the next generation?

CULTURE

*What you see and
what you feel*

DAY 17

An Intentional Culture
Churches must be intentional about designing and creating healthy church cultures.

A FEW YEARS ago I entered a Gothic-style mainline church in one of Canada's leading cities for the wedding of some good friends of mine. I knew a number of other friends would be in attendance, and all of us were excited to reconnect.

As I walked up the steps, I met some old friends. We greeted each other and continued into the church. Before I could sit down, more friends greeted me, and we conversed happily for a few moments. I settled down on a church pew, and while I waited for the ceremony to start, I greeted yet other long-term friends. One of my favorite parts of weddings has always been the chance to see good friends and build closer relationships, and what better place to do that than in the church?

Suddenly, the minister walked across the stage and shouted from the altar: "Be quiet in here! This is the house of God."

I was shocked. Clearly, in all innocence, we had violated a church culture that was unfamiliar to us. There was no room for conversation in this place. I quietly folded my arms, wondering what I was allowed to do or say. Connecting with people is one of the things church does best. We are members of a family, and it's logical and healthy for there to be expressions of joy when we see each other. I realized with sadness that their culture was actually disconnecting people from the church family they needed.

Unfortunately, many churches are little more than places for baby dedications, weddings, and funerals—a place for the "hatched, matched, and dispatched." The problem isn't with the gospel. It's with the culture.

Culture is a powerful—yet often underestimated—part of church life. A toxic, non-relational culture has the power to drive away the people who most need to know God and find family. On the other hand, a welcoming, authentic culture can facilitate God's work in people's hearts. Developing a healthy church culture is one of the most important things a church can do.

THE POWER OF CULTURE

When it comes to our day-to-day lives and our social interactions, it is easy to recognize the influence of culture. We observe its existence and power everywhere we look:

1. The culture of a *country* is created by the beliefs and values of its people. Every nation has unique customs, social expressions, history, and ways of treating one another.
2. The culture in a *city* is determined by the economic conditions, the laws that govern the people, and its ethnic and social makeup.
3. Individual *neighborhoods* have their own culture. For example, there could be a family culture, a university culture, or a party culture.
4. The culture in a *family* is determined by its core beliefs, the rules of family life, and how the parents put their beliefs into practice.

Just as countries, cities, neighborhoods, and families have cultures, every church has its own culture. Culture is what you see and feel when you enter a church. It is the attitude of the people and the environment they create. It is the way of life within that church: how people act, how they treat each other, and how they relate to God.

Generally, a culture either attracts you or repels you; it draws you in or pushes you away. I've heard it said that a person decides within fifteen minutes of entering a church whether to return. A healthy culture in a church will attract people and help them respond to God and His Word.

BY DESIGN OR DEFAULT?

How should church culture be developed? In his book *By Design or Default?*, Kevin Gerald, pastor of Champion Centre in Tacoma, Washington, says, "Church culture is most often created by default." Clearly, the culture of the cathedral I visited that day had been shaped by many years of religion; as a result, it may have intimidated and driven people away. I remember thinking, *I never want to enter or attend a church like this again.* That is the opposite of what we want people to feel when they attend church!

Culture needs to be intentional. It should create an environment that welcomes people, makes them feel included, encourages them to contribute, and produces within them a desire to return.

Who is responsible for the design of church culture? Is culture designed by God, or is it created by leaders? Sitting in the church pew that day, I asked myself that question. Did God design a culture of intimidation and fear? Or was this non-relational atmosphere the accidental result of countless years of customs, rules, and rituals?

A friend of mine named Gabe, who was born and raised in Mexico, recently told me he experienced culture shock when he visited my home in Canada. As is common in our country, he was invited to remove his shoes upon entering the house. He told me that was initially quite a shock to him, because in his culture, you would never remove your shoes to enter a home. To us, it seemed natural; but to our guest, it was a foreign, uncomfortable experience. Unfortunately, it's easy for even well-meaning church leaders to neglect culture. We get so familiar with our routines and so busy doing the work of the ministry that we forget to consider how first-time guests feel when they enter our church buildings, hear our messages, or sing our songs.

A healthy culture in a family is taught and shaped by the parents. In the same way, a healthy culture in a church is first the responsibility of its leaders. Church culture is defined by the decisions leaders make, the quality of life that is created, the beliefs and values that are fostered, and the way people are taught to treat one another.

One of the things I appreciate about my son, Pastor Jachin, and the team of leaders we have in our church is the value they place on intentionally building culture. This wasn't even a topic of conversation in my generation of leaders, so the leaders of the next generation church took on the task of setting seven "culture targets" that became the guidelines for the language and environment of Home Church.

In the next few chapters, we will look at each of these cultural values in more detail. We are indebted to Pastor Kevin Gerald of Champion Centre in Tacoma, Washington, for these seven values which we have adopted as our own. They have become an essential part of our church.

When our church leadership became intentional about designing the kind of culture we wanted, it was much easier to foster and form that culture. But leaders aren't the only ones responsible for church culture: every person who considers a church their home should adopt and promote the culture of the house. Just like children are responsible to respond to their parents' values and way of living, so a church family should work together to create a unified, healthy atmosphere.

There is no such thing as a perfect culture or an ideal culture which every church must imitate. Just like each family is unique, so each church has its own environment, calling, and values. The key is for both leaders and members to discover God's plan for their church and do everything they can to design and foster a sound cultural environment.

As churches align themselves with God's calling for their culture, they will create a healthy environment where people want to belong.

THINGS TO THINK ABOUT

1. Why do you think church culture is important?

2. What are some things you could do to foster and promote the culture of your church?

3. How have you shifted your personal culture to align with the culture of your church? What areas still need some work to become aligned?

Chad's Story

As a child, poverty was a huge part of my life. My mom was sixteen and my dad was nineteen when I was born, so they had nothing. There was some food, but it was less than basic. I remember sifting maggots from flour to make pancakes and not being bothered by it. We always made the most of what we had, but poverty had a grip on me. Stealing was justified in my mind because I had nothing. Learning to be generous is tough when you think everyone should give to you.

Abuse was also a normal part of my life. I loved my dad but loathed when he would come home late, usually under the influence of alcohol. He would always get in a fight with Mom. I became very angry and resentful and had lots of struggles because of it.

The sitters who used to look after us were fun to start with but turned out to be perverted and sexually abusive. Darkness filled our home. I was so ashamed of being fondled and coerced to do things I did not want to do. I became very self-conscious. I lacked confidence in my teens because of the battle in my mind.

I used to watch my dad have a great time with his friends doing drugs around the coffee table. I looked forward to being old enough to join him and have fun. I was so naive I took my dad's hash knives to third grade show-and-tell and taught the kids how to smoke hash. It's no wonder my friends were not allowed to stay over. And my dad wasn't very happy with me that day either. As a child I didn't know what normal was.

Pornography was my secret pleasure from a young age. When I was eight years old, I found Playboy magazines in the closet. Soon it became my addiction. There was a very effective hiding spot in the attic of our house where I would spend hours looking at dirty magazines. I lived in a fantasy world.

I look back now at the road I was on, and I can't even imagine where I would be today if everything hadn't changed at the age of twelve. That was when I asked God to help me.

The first time I stepped through the doors of a church, it was a youth meeting. The message was so impactful and full of life. I was very worldly, but several people began to mentor and teach a few of us young men. Thank you, Rick, Craig, and Theo! It was a small part of my life at the time, but it became the new direction for the rest of my life.

When I was thirteen, my mom and dad split up. We had to move in a hurry from our small town into the city to get away. The only option we had was the women's shelter. My mom is such a warrior. She got us through that time, again with the help and guidance of church friends.

The most critical decision at that stage of my life was to begin attending a Christian school. For me it was a safe zone and a new start. Very quickly I realized this school wasn't just about learning—it was about caring, mentoring, parenting, healing, and much more! Now it wasn't just my mom trying to get us to make godly decisions. It was the whole community of the church.

I still had lots of issues, and my parents were in the middle of a divorce. I became a vagabond, trying to find a place to stay so I could go to school. Both Mom and Dad lived forty-five minutes away and could not take me, so I constantly moved from one host home to another. I probably interrupted many people's lives, but I was desperate for this new life.

I became a church mouse. The church truly was my home. Whenever I could be at church, I would go. I learned to serve, to share stories of my life, and to help others. I didn't know it at the time, but I was making lifelong decisions when I decided to plant myself in the local church.

Now, twenty-plus years later, I look at my life, my wife, and my two beautiful kids, and I know that without the church, I would not be where I am now. I found my purpose, I found my calling, I found my home. I have so many people to thank who have been part of my life and have helped peel the layers of darkness away, showing me how to live a full and happy life.

My high school basketball teammates are now my lifelong friends. We have kids who are growing up together and playing on the same sports teams we played on (Go Warriors!). It brings me great joy to know my teenage kids won't have to deal with the kinds of things I had to deal with, and if they ever need anything, they are surrounded by people who love them and want the best for them.

DAY 18

An Honor Culture
Honor is a way of life.

HONOR IS THE way we treat one another and the way we live out our lives. It is a choice we make in every relationship.

Years ago, I faced a dilemma regarding how to honor my father. My father had a mental disorder when I was a child, and he was placed in a mental institution for about a year. One day my mother arranged for him to attend healing services in our local church, and he was marvelously healed by God's power. Despite his physical healing, he never really learned how to be a dad or how to mentor his sons. He was present in the home, he provided for his family, he was faithful to his church and read the Bible every day—but he never developed a close relationship with his kids. In my book *Be a Man,* I describe this absentee relationship and its effects on me.

When he retired he became ill again. He was on the wrong medications, and tragically he ended his life in suicide. I'll never forget the phone call from my sister informing me our father had hanged himself on a rope in her garage. I was thirty-one years old at the time.

My father's suicide, along with the many years of distance in our relationship, left me with a choice: would I be honoring toward my father? He chose a death many would call dishonorable. Would I choose to honor or dishonor his life and legacy?

I was familiar with Ephesians 6:3, which says, "If you honor your father and mother, 'things will go well for you, and you will have a long life on the earth'" (NKJV). I made a conscious decision to practice honor. I placed a headstone on his burial site engraved with the words, "Honorable husband, father, granddad."

Honor is a command in Scripture. It is a God-established principle of life, not something subject to our circumstances or emotions.

HONOR GOD

Our honor begins with God. We honor God when we give Him our first and our best. The book of Malachi in the Old Testament gives us a negative example of honoring God. It describes how God's people gave offerings from the blind, crippled, and diseased animals, even though God had told them they were to give Him the best of the flock. God was displeased and refused to accept their offerings (Malachi 1:6-14).

Matthew 6:33 tells us, "Seek first his kingdom and his righteousness, and all these things will be given to you as well" (NIV). We should ask ourselves, "Do I regularly honor God by giving Him the first and best of my time and resources? Do I give God my tithe, which is ten percent of my income?"

We all want the favor of God in our lives; however, favor is often the result of putting God first and giving Him our best. That doesn't mean we earn His favor or deserve His blessings, of course. His grace is free, His mercies are undeserved, and His favor is far beyond what we could ask, expect, or imagine. When we honor Him, though, we declare our faith in Him and our commitment to His commands. God honors faith and obedience; therefore, in response to our faith, He pours out far greater measures of favor than we deserve.

HONOR AUTHORITY

Our honor begins with God and then extends to the authorities in our lives. The Bible says, "Honor all people. Love the brotherhood. Fear God. Honor the king" (1 Peter 2:17). Honor and respect are to be given to parents (Ephesians 6:1-3), to government leaders (Romans 13:1-2), to church leaders (1 Timothy 2:1-2), and to others who have authority over us.

A young man at the Los Angeles Dream Center once asked me, "How can I honor my dad when I've never met him?" I explained honor isn't earned or deserved but rather *given* by him to his father, who made his life possible.

The Bible also teaches that leaders in God's house should be honored and esteemed for the work they do. Paul wrote, "Dear brothers and sisters, honor those who are your leaders in the Lord's work. They work hard among you and give you spiritual guidance. Show them great respect and wholehearted love because of their work" (1 Thessalonians 5:12-13).

HONOR EVERYONE

Honor is one of the basic needs of every human being. Everyone needs to feel respected, no matter their station or status in life. Self-esteem is built into people's lives by the words others speak to them.

Scripture teaches the principle that followers of Jesus should think of others more highly than themselves. "Don't be selfish; don't try to impress others. Be humble, thinking of others as better than yourselves" (Philippians 2:3). This doesn't mean we ignore our own needs or allow abusive situations to continue. It means we genuinely value other people. It is an others-focused way of thinking and living rather than a self-focused one.

HONOR IN THE CHURCH

Honor in the house of God means everyone is to be honored, from the greatest leader to the youngest child. Maybe you've been to a church where the only people who received honor were the leader and a few elite others. A church culture with honor makes *everyone* feel accepted and loved.

The culture of every church should be a culture of honor. A statement that Home Church has adopted is, "Honor up, honor down, honor all around." Everyone is honored, from the youngest child in the nursery to the most senior adult.

A young man named Ryan shared his story with me a while back. Ryan told me how he came from a culture where people got ahead by tearing others down. In his circle of friends, those with the quickest comebacks and the best put-downs were the most admired. At his job, people got ahead by making others look bad. Even in his experiences with sports, players would get more playing time by making other players look bad.

When he came to Home Church, he witnessed something he had never seen before: real honor. He was amazed at how spouses treated each other. They didn't call each other names like "my old lady" or make fun of each other. Friends treated each other well. They were respected and admired among their peers not because they put each other down, but because they lifted each other up and encouraged one another to reach their full potential in Christ.

Ryan said watching this real love in action changed him in a profound way. It was the opposite of everything he had ever been taught. You don't step on people when they are down—you help them get up. He began to find joy and excitement in encouraging others. Choosing to honor is now a way of life for Ryan and his family, and he finds genuine fulfillment in watching others succeed.

An honor culture is a healthy culture because honor adds value to people. In every area of our lives—homes, workplaces, churches—we should be people who show honor. As a result, the favor of God will be on our lives in a greater way, and we will be a blessing everywhere we go.

THINGS TO THINK ABOUT

1. What does the word "honor" mean to you?

2. What are some practical ways you can show honor to people in your life?

A *Relationship Culture*
Developing relationships is a lifelong process.

I MENTIONED EARLIER that in my travels, I often ask people this question: "What percentage of your relationship with God comes through your relationship with one another?" In other words, to what extent does the church community—including worship, prayer, preaching, prophecy, and counsel—help facilitate people's walk with God?

The answer is consistently around sixty percent. On average more than half of our relationship with God is developed through a proper relationship with one another. Yes, we meet God and hear from God on our own; but one-on-one communication is only part of our walk with Him. To a great extent, we need the people around us to help us draw closer to God. Community is a natural, healthy, and effective way to strengthen our relationship with God.

The church is built both on a relationship with God and a relationship with one another. We could visualize this threefold relationship like a triangle with God at the apex and you and me on the bottom angles. The closer you and I get to God, the closer we get to one another. You can't draw closer to God without getting closer to other people in the process.

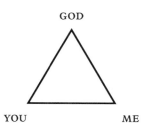

GOD

YOU   ME

A relationship culture in the family of God refers to how people connect, interact, and treat one another. When a relationship culture is built upon an honor culture, interpersonal interactions are positive, wholesome, and edifying. In an atmosphere of honor, people can genuinely express their love and appreciation for one another. Church becomes a "mutual admiration society" where people are built up, lifted up, and encouraged to become the people God has called them to be.

The relationship culture God has established in His Word could be called a "one another" culture. The Bible refers to our interpersonal connections using this phrase numerous times. Here are a few of the *one anothers* of Scripture.

1. *Love one another.*

> A new command I give you: Love one another. As I have loved you, so you must love one another. By this everyone will know that you are my disciples, if you love one another.
> (John 13:34-35 NIV)

People should say of every church, "See how they love one another!" By definition, love is directed toward other people. Love is more than an emotion: it is a decision to focus on and invest ourselves in others, including our spouses, our families, our friends, and even people we've never met. Love is intentional about serving and giving to others. God demonstrated this kind of intentional love toward us: "But God showed his great love for us by sending Christ to die for us while we were still sinners" (Romans 5:8).

Love in the church starts with Jesus. Jesus loved us so much that He gave Himself to save us and to establish us in a wholesome, healthy church family filled with great relationships.

Our love is to be like God's love, which is described in the Bible using the Greek word *agape*. This term refers to a love that is greater than human love. When a person says, "I fell in love," he or she is referring to human love. This is a wonderful love, because it describes human attraction and connection. However, agape love is even greater. Agape love stretches like a canopy to cover a multitude of faults, failures, and sins in others. "Most important of all, continue to show deep love for each other, for love covers a multitude of sins" (1 Peter 4:8).

2. *Forgive one another.*

> Bear with each other and forgive one another if any of you has a grievance against someone. Forgive as the Lord forgave you.
> (Colossians 3:13 NIV)

To forgive means to let go of the offenses we tend to collect along life's journey. The potential to get offended is a part of life—Jesus Himself said offenses would exist and we would need to practice forgiveness. Ongoing forgiveness is one of the primary keys to a wholesome life.

Ask yourself these questions: Are you holding a grudge against anyone right now? How long does it take you to forgive people who have offended you? The answers will help you evaluate whether you have learned to live in forgiveness.

I remember on one occasion, Heather and I had begun to harbor bitterness in our hearts toward certain people over some unresolved issues. We felt like God said to us, "If you do not forgive, your future is over." It was a serious wake-up call. We realized practicing forgiveness—even toward someone who had not asked for it—was important for our future. Had we not learned the habit of quick forgiveness, we would probably be bitter, grudge-holding people right now. Instead, we don't feel like we have an enemy in the world. We love life, love people, and love the church.

I think the highest form of forgiveness is when you choose to forgive someone *before* he or she repents and asks for forgiveness. That is a direct manifestation of God's grace because grace is unmerited and unconditional. As we follow Jesus, God gives us this level of grace toward other people.

3. Accept one another.

> Accept one another, then, just as Christ accepted you, in order to bring praise to God.
> (Romans 15:7 NIV)

We are to accept, receive, and welcome one another as God has accepted us. This acceptance allows us to build spiritual family relationships with one another. In many cases, especially when a person's home environment is dysfunctional, friendships within the house of God become some of the most meaningful, healthy relationships a person can experience.

That is the power of spiritual adoption—inviting people who have been alienated into a spiritual family. God accepts us this way, and His acceptance provides a model for how we are to accept others. When we are "born again," we become children of God, immediately adopted into His family, equally accepted with all the children of God.

4. Esteem one another.

> Let nothing be done through selfish ambition or conceit, but in lowliness of mind let each esteem others better than himself.
> (Philippians 2:3 NKJV)

Esteem has to do with the high regard we have for each other. Another word for it is honor, which we looked at in the previous chapter. Esteeming one another means to choose to think and speak positively about one another.

Referring to church leaders, God tells us to "esteem them very highly in love for their work's sake" (1 Thessalonians 5:13). In other words, we are to give honor to whom honor is due. Their labor is valuable and deserves recognition.

5. Edify one another.

> Therefore comfort each other and edify one another, just as you also are doing.
> (1 Thessalonians 5:11 NKJV)

The word *edify* could also be translated "to build up." It simply means discovering where someone is at in the development of life and then adding something that advances the building process. It is like building a house: you begin with the foundation, then you erect the walls, then you build a roof, then you finish the construction, and finally you furnish it. Every step is necessary and beautiful in its own way, and the finished product is something everyone can enjoy.

God designed relationships in His family to be positive. It is our responsibility to seek the things that contribute to growth and edification, rather than destruction. "A wise woman builds her home, but a foolish woman tears it down with her own hands" (Proverbs 14:1).

In particular, our words have the power to build up or tear down. Proverbs says it this way: "The tongue can bring death or life; those who love to talk will reap the consequences" (Proverbs 18:21). There is no place for condemnation, bullying, or other verbal expressions that tear people down.

6. Comfort one another.

As we read earlier, 1 Thessalonians 5:11 says, "comfort each other and edify one another." To comfort means to enter into the pain of another person and bring solace, healing, and hope.

We are not to be like Job's "comforters," who tried to find some reason to blame him for the tragedies he experienced. Rather than comforting him, they accused him, questioned him, misjudged him, and hurt him. Job finally said in exasperation, "I have heard all this before. What miserable comforters you are!" (Job 16:2). Ultimately God confronted Job's friends for their words.

On a side note: at the end of the story, God told Job to pray for His friends because they had not spoken correctly about God. When Job did, God blessed him with twice as much as he had before. God will reward us for our proper response in the face of unfair criticism or other relational conflicts. It's worth it to respond in love and humility.

Rather than being "miserable comforters," our goal is to come alongside hurting people with humility and patience. We usually won't have all the answers, but our unconditional love and acceptance will give people strength. God is in charge of their healing, and our role is to provide a safe place throughout that process.

7. Encourage one another.

> And let us not neglect our meeting together, as some people do, but encourage one another, especially now that the day of his return is drawing near.
> (Hebrews 10:25)

Encouragement refers to giving someone the courage he or she needs to face the tests and circumstances of life. "You're going to make it" and "God will see you through" are important phrases in your relationship vocabulary.

God always sees beyond where we are right now. He can give us perspective not only about our own lives, but about others as well. Often He uses us to encourage other people to move into their future.

I often tell people, "greatness is in your future." God said to Abraham, "I will make you into a great nation, and I will bless you; I will make your name great, and you will be a blessing" (Genesis 12:2). We are all children of Abraham; therefore, we all have greatness in our future—not failure but success, and not smallness but largeness.

Using our words to bring hope and faith is one of the most exciting benefits of living in community. Always be on the lookout for people you can speak words of life to. Often your encouraging words will be exactly what they needed to hear in the moment.

8. Think good thoughts toward one another.

For me, thinking good thoughts toward another person often means thinking about the good things God has in store for that person's future. He sees their potential, not just who they are today. God always thinks positive thoughts about you. Because He has big plans for you, He thinks greater thoughts about you than you think about yourself.

When God found Moses, he was depressed, he was wandering in the wilderness, and he had a stuttering problem. But that's not how God saw him. He saw him as the leader who would take the children of Israel to the Promised Land. When God found Gideon, he was hiding from the enemy in a winepress, trying to thresh grain out of sight. But God saw him as a mighty warrior and called him to deliver His people from the enemy. God had bigger and better thoughts about Moses and Gideon than they did about themselves. God saw the leadership potential in them, and He sees it in all of us too.

Whenever I am with people, I have a personal, unspoken goal: I want them to feel better about themselves and their future after my connection with them. Every interaction with others is an opportunity to build people and build the house of God.

The power of relationship cannot be underestimated. Your relationships with people either move them forward or backward—and move you forward or backward too. Your love, forgiveness, acceptance, esteem, edification, comfort, and encouragement affirm the greatness people often do not see within themselves.

THINGS TO THINK ABOUT

1. Rate your "one another" relationship practices on a scale of 1-10, where 1 is the lowest and 10 is the highest.

Love one another	( )
Forgive one another	( )
Accept one another	( )
Esteem one another	( )
Edify one another	( )
Comfort one another	( )
Encourage one another	( )
Think good thoughts toward one another	( )

2. Which one had the lowest score? Write down a couple of practical, tangible ways you could improve in that area.

Barb's Story

When I was five years old, my neighbor invited our family to church. My mom and new stepfather declined, but my neighbor persisted and asked if she could take us children. My siblings also declined at first, but I said yes. So the following week, they picked me up and took me to church.

I loved it from the very beginning. I heard how much God loved me and how He gave His only Son for me. I determined from the very first week that since Jesus had given His life for me, I would live the rest of my life for Him.

It soon become painfully obvious that the other children there always came with their parents. I was the only kid without a family. For a while that bothered me, but over time I just became "theirs." It was like I was the child the whole church was helping love, raise, and nurture. I didn't realize it at the time, but this act of "group adoption" began to shape something in my mind and heart: the church was my home, and the people in the church were my family. I no longer felt awkward or lonely, but instead I knew I had many moms I could go to for help.

Today, I am a pastor, a wife, and a mother of four children of my own—but the church is still my home and my family. God promises to set the lonely in families, and He does that through His family, which is the church.

A Worship Culture
Man was created by God to worship
"in spirit and in truth."

I WILL NEVER forget my first real worship experience because it radically changed my personal relationship with God. I was raised in a Christian church that followed what you could call a "traditional" form of worship. We sang hymns and choruses, and although mentally I agreed with what I was singing, I never really connected with God in tangible worship. This continued to be the case even after I graduated from Bible college and entered the ministry.

At age twenty-two, however, my life was about to change. I became very hungry for the Holy Spirit. I found myself desperately desiring more of God in my life. I began to hear of a great movement of the Holy Spirit that was affecting thousands of people and churches, including many historical churches. Evangelicals and Catholics alike were receiving the amazing experience of the baptism with the Holy Spirit and the spiritual gift of speaking in tongues.

I attended some of the meetings, and I noticed the predominant characteristic was a different flow of worship than I was used to. People were singing corporately in the Spirit. I remembered the Scripture that says, "I will sing in the spirit, and I will also sing in words I understand" (1 Corinthians 14:15). I listened to the people sing and then break out in audible praise to God, flowing together in beautiful harmony. The presence of God seemed to be felt in a greater way as the people sang in the Spirit.

Cautiously, I began participating in the services. The songs that were sung in that era were often Bible verses put to music. I joined in and lifted my hands in worship. Then, at the end of one of the songs, I opened my mouth and began singing in harmony with the hundreds of people that were present.

Suddenly something happened. I felt my spirit being set free. One of the songs that was popular at the time included these lyrics: "Set my spirit free that I might worship Thee / Set my spirit free that I might praise Thy name / Let all bondage go and let deliverance flow / Set my spirit free to worship Thee" (Charlotte Baker, © 1975). The words of that song became my reality, and my spirit was set free like a bird from a cage. My heart found the intimacy with God I had been longing for, and from that day forward, I have enjoyed a depth and reality of worship that is hard to put into words.

The following year we arrived in the city of Red Deer, Alberta. From the very beginning, worship was a vital part of the church we planted. Honoring God through worship was the norm, and we saw many people's lives changed as they encountered God in authentic, heartfelt worship.

Today Home Church continues to value and foster worship as one of our core values. We begin and end every service with worship, and everyone is invited to participate. We are intentional about creating an environment where people of all ages can experience God personally. Styles of music have changed, new songs are constantly being written, technology is different, and the stage and building are geared toward a younger culture—but the heart of worship hasn't changed. Church is still a place where finite humans can encounter the infinite God and be transformed in His presence.

DESIGNED TO WORSHIP

Humans were designed to worship. It springs from within us: from a God-created desire to be connected to Him.

Everyone will worship someone or something. Religions typically worship specific gods or spirits; many people, however, worship the god of self. Self is perhaps the greatest false god our modern civilization follows and serves. Ironically, though, the only way to find true and lasting fulfillment is to turn our eyes beyond ourselves and worship the one true God.

Worship is the yielding of self to a greater power. When you worship, you turn your focus from yourself and give God the honor that belongs to Him. As Christians, our allegiance is to the God of the universe, Jesus Christ Himself, who is Lord of all.

Worship must be a genuine expression of the heart. It cannot be lip service or empty emotion—it must be real. Jesus said, "true worshipers will worship the Father in spirit and in truth" (John 4:23). True worship is more than music or songs. It is a heart attitude of surrender, gratitude, and admiration toward God. Expressing your heart to God and singing in the Spirit releases your life to God and allows you to connect with Him on a spiritual level.

The Bible says, "Enter his gates with thanksgiving; go into his courts with praise. Give thanks to him and praise his name" (Psalm 100:4). This is the reason we begin our church services with praise and worship, thanking God for what He has done for us during the past week.

EXPRESSIONS OF WORSHIP

If we truly worship God in our hearts, we will express it outwardly. Singing and praying are clear examples of this, of course. So are clapping, raising our hands, dancing, and other outward expressions of our passion for God. David wrote, "Because your steadfast love is better than life, my lips will praise you. So I will bless you as long as I live; in your name I will lift up my hands" (Psalm 63:3–4 ESV). Paul wrote to the Ephesians about "singing psalms and hymns and spiritual songs among yourselves, and making music to the Lord in your hearts" (Ephesians 5:19).

Generosity is a form of worship as well. When the wise men found Jesus as a young child, they worshiped Him and gave Him gifts. Giving your resources—time, money, talents, material possessions—to God is worship.

Gratitude is another manifestation of a worshipful heart. When we recognize all God has done for us, we naturally want to express our thanks to Him. One time Jesus healed ten lepers, but only one (who happened to be a foreigner) returned to thank Him. That clearly made Jesus sad. He said to the one who returned, "Didn't I heal ten men? Where are the other nine? Has no one returned to give glory to God?" (Luke 17:17). We must make sure we are part of the percentage that gives Jesus praise for all He has done.

Worship is not just something you do for a few minutes during a church service. You can worship God, including with prayer and singing, not only at church, but also in private: at home, on the road, outdoors, or wherever you are able to take a few moments to thank and praise Him.

INTENSE PRAISE

There are times we need to become more expressive in extraordinary praise to God. After all, what He has done for us deserves great praise and thanksgiving.

Moses' sister, Miriam, picked up a tambourine and led the people in a celebratory dance in the desert. Why? Because the nation, which had only days prior been miraculously delivered from slavery in Egypt, once again witnessed God's intervention on their behalf when Pharaoh's army tried to recapture them. God brought them safely across the Red Sea, and then the Egyptians were defeated while trying to chase them down. The people of Israel were so filled with joy over what God had done for them that they began to sing and dance. Their years of tyranny were over, and they were beginning a new life, thanks to God's grace and power.

Likewise, we have been delivered from the tyranny of sin and set free to follow God into His promises and blessings. Praise and worship are natural, heartfelt expressions of gratitude for all God has done for us. Worship is a faith declaration that our best days are ahead as we continue to follow God throughout our lives.

THINGS TO THINK ABOUT

1. In what ways do you usually express worship to God?

2. What benefits of worship have you seen in your own life?

DAY 21

A Generous Culture
Giving is about more than money:
it is an attitude for life.

MY MOTHER TAUGHT my siblings and me the principle of tithing when we were young. I remember her showing us a one-dollar bill, then breaking it down into ten dimes and explaining that God expected each of us to give back to Him ten percent of the money we received.

I remember giving God the tithe of my first income check when I was fourteen years old. It was natural for me to do that because I had been taught that giving is not just about money—it is an attitude toward life, God, and material possessions. The result has been a lifetime of blessings.

Generosity lies at the very foundation of Christianity: God so loved us that He *gave* His only begotten Son (John 3:16). When Jesus comes into our hearts, our automatic, love-inspired response is to give our time, talents, and material resources for His use. A generous culture is normal for Christians who have been touched by God's amazing grace and love. He deserves the first and the best, not the leftovers of life. Jesus gave His all for us, so how could we not give our all to Him?

WHAT GOD WILL DO

God gives us many blessings out of sheer grace and love, but when we practice the principle of tithing, He goes above and beyond. He commits to bless us supernaturally and abundantly because He loves cheerful, willing givers (2 Corinthians 9:7).

God demonstrates this commitment in the "I will" statements of Malachi 3:8-12. When God said, "I will," He made a promise to us. If we believe His promise and practice the teachings of His Word, He will be faithful to fulfill His end of the promise. When we give our tithes and offerings—when we are tithers, not just tippers—God obligates Himself to fulfill His promises regarding our finances.

1. God promises to provide for us: "I will open the windows of heaven for you" (verse 10).
2. God promises to prosper us: "I will pour out a blessing so great you won't have enough room to take it in" (verse 10).
3. God promises to protect us: "I will guard [your crops] from insects and disease. Your grapes will not fall from the vine before they are ripe" (verse 11).
4. God promises to promote us: "Then all nations will call you blessed" (verse 12).

STEWARDSHIP OF LIFE

We are *stewards* and *managers* of our lives, not *owners*. In other words, we recognize that everything we are and everything we have is a gift from God. Our resources are "on loan" to us, and we are responsible to use them wisely and for His kingdom. Stewardship is the systematic giving of time, talents, and material possessions to God.

Giving to those in need, beyond our tithes, is an excellent way to steward the money God has entrusted to us. At Home Church, hundreds of people give to the poor through various ministries and giving opportunities. Their gifts help lift the poor out of the dust and make them princes (1 Samuel 2:8). As I mentioned earlier, years ago Heather and I began giving to an orphan boy in India named Robert. From his beginning in the poverty-stricken streets of India, we have watched and celebrated as Robert received an education, became a nurse, and went on to become one of the main leaders in our churches in India.

Giving our time, talents, and energy is the reflection of a culture of generosity. As a follower of Jesus, investing whatever time I can in God's kingdom has always been a joy for me. My life is not a forty-hour work week, but a life of giving extra and doing extra for God's kingdom. If I were not a full-time pastor, I would still show up at church early to welcome people, invite visitors out for lunch, make disciples, and do the work of the ministry.

As a church we do not hesitate to invite people to voluntarily contribute their time, talents, and financial resources. If we do not ask people to give, we deprive them of God's blessing. The Bible says, "Give freely and become more wealthy; be stingy and lose everything. The generous will prosper; those who refresh others will themselves be refreshed" (Proverbs 11:24-25).

To live in the blessing of God is the most wonderful life. How wonderful to have a job that is the result of God's blessing; how wonderful to be part of a family that lives under God's blessing; how wonderful to belong to a church that is blessed by God; and how wonderful to give and sacrifice so churches can be planted all over the world and the good news of Jesus can go forward!

My generation has had the privilege of providing for the generation to come, just as each generation before mine did and each generation after mine will do. Giving is an investment in the future of the next generation. It is also an investment in our future life in heaven, because God will reward us someday for how we use our earthly goods. Both *heaven* and *souls* are eternal investments, unlike earthly investments. What better way to use our resources than to invest them in things that will never fade away or be lost?

THINGS TO THINK ABOUT

1. Are you committed to a lifestyle of giving through your tithe, time, and talents?

2. What benefits have you seen in your life from this commitment?

3. What specific generosity goals would you like to set and reach in your life?

Raju's Story

Raju Tamang, the pastor of Home Church Chennai's Nepali location, was born and raised in the nation of Bhutan. Raju was the eldest in a family of Nepali descent.

In 1990, while studying at an engineering college, Raju joined an illegal student-led political movement to bring freedom and change in Bhutan. Shortly thereafter, he was arrested. He spent two and a half years in prison, where he was tortured and watched many of his friends die.

When he was released, he was bitter and broken from his prison experience. He was angry at God, and he questioned how God could allow such a thing to happen in his life. Out of frustration, Raju cried out to every god he could think of, including Hindu gods, Buddha, and Christ. He said, "Whichever god answers me will be the god I believe in and serve." But he heard nothing.

After two months Raju received a great opportunity. A Norwegian woman, a Christian missionary doctor to Bhutan who had befriended him while he was imprisoned, offered to pay his schooling expenses and send him to school in Chennai, South India.

After two years of studies, Raju became friends with several young men and women who were part of Youth With A Mission in Chennai. One night, when Raju was very sick, several of these young men came to his home to pray for him. Raju received an instantaneous, miraculous healing and made the decision to finally say yes to Jesus.

That evening Raju could not stop thinking about the decision he had made. Was it the correct decision? Had he been too hasty? He was unable to sleep. As he lay awake, the Lord took him back to the moment two years earlier when he had cried out to all the "gods." Here was Jesus, the only one who had answered him, reminding him of what He had said. His decision to believe and follow Christ was confirmed. Christ brought a complete conviction to his life that night and began transforming his life.

In 2000 Raju married a beautiful woman named Romila. God has given them three wonderful children. In 2007 Raju resigned his position at an IT company in Chennai and began the process of applying for resettlement in the United States as an asylum seeker.

At this time of transition, Raju and Romila's lives were intersected with a clear call of God to go into the ministry as pastors. The process of resettlement was put on hold. Raju and Romila started a church in Chennai among the thousands of Nepali-speaking people who lived there.

The church grew quickly, and soon they needed a better facility to meet in. Then Raju and Romila met Pastors Shawn and Sheralyn Acheson, who were pastoring Home Church's English-speaking location in Chennai. The Achesons immediately invited the Nepali church to meet in their building. Raju and Romila were amazed as they listened to the teaching on church DNA, core values, and cultural targets, and they knew Home Church was what was needed for Chennai and especially the Nepali-speaking people of the city.

After sharing Home Church's facility for a year, the Nepali-speaking church made the choice to become Home Church. The decision had been confirmed by the life-giving, authentic relationship that had formed between the two church families.

As Home Church pastors, Raju and Romila have adopted the church's beliefs, values, culture, structures, and systems, which has resulted in the growth of their location. These church principles have helped the church grow relationally and have taught ways of building a better church for people looking to find Christ. This has resulted in great church growth among the Nepali community in Chennai. The Home Church location in Chennai now runs two full Sunday experiences every week, and they recently have launched a church for the Nepali community in the city of Kerala, in the neighboring state.

DAY 22

A Volunteer Culture
Volunteerism means 100 percent of the people do 100 percent of the work.

IN A FUNCTIONAL family, everyone—whether small or great—contributes to the well-being and success of the family. Everyone has tasks, responsibilities, gifts, and talents that work together to build the family.

The church is the family of God, and, as such, everyone should feel called and empowered to contribute to the wellbeing of the house of God. In a volunteer culture, everyone is given the vision, opportunity, and tools to serve. The family is strengthened by the cooperation and contribution of each member.

Volunteerism can be spelled w-o-r-k. Here's an acronym that describes some key characteristics of an effective volunteer.

w   *Willing*
o   *On Time*
r   *Responsible*
k   *Kingdom-Focused*

Willing
Volunteers love what they do, because all effective service flows from a servant heart. A volunteer culture means people are more concerned about the health of the house than the exercise of their gift, recognition, or power. True volunteers don't need to force

themselves into a position or be forced to accept a position. They simply serve where the opportunity and need are greatest. Usually, though, their gift soon creates space for them (see Proverbs 16:18), and they find a role they feel comfortable with in the life and flow of the church.

On Time

Punctuality is no minor thing: it is essential to effective teamwork. It communicates that you respect and value other people's schedules and plans. When people are counting on you to arrive at a certain time, to have things ready before a meeting starts, or to meet a deadline, a lack of promptness can greatly affect the outcome of many people's work. I remember one church where a wonderful person with an amazing gift to work with children had been serving. However, being punctual was such an issue that her responsibilities suffered and other people began to be affected. Eventually, she had to be removed from the team and a replacement had to be found. Her talent and gift went unused because she couldn't manage her schedule.

Responsible

Responsibility means ownership. It means picking up a load and carrying it to the end rather than dropping it halfway through. Lamentations 3:27 says, "It is good for a man to bear the yoke while he is young" (NIV). Make the task yours and see it through to the end.

Kingdom-Focused

As followers of Jesus, our focus is on Him. We want His will to be done and His kingdom to come. That means approaching each task with a sense of importance and urgency. Whatever we do, no matter how small it may seem, is significant to God's plan on Earth.

VOLUNTEER-DRIVEN CHURCHES

There are two kinds of churches: staff-driven churches, where the staff does most of the work of building the church; and volunteer-driven churches, where the staff focuses on raising up volunteers to do the work of the ministry. I believe a volunteer-driven church is the New Testament model.

Ephesians 4:11-12 says, "So Christ himself gave the apostles, the prophets, the evangelists, the pastors and teachers, to equip his people for works of service" (NIV). These five ministries are not called to do all the work of ministry but rather to teach, train, model, and release people to serve.

The volunteer church is not a self-focused church where people want to find "their" ministry. That kind of attitude becomes toxic very quickly. A true servant cares about the health and success of the church, not just his or her own ministry.

A volunteer-based church is a church where people have an attitude of service that goes beyond a title or position. This was the perspective Jesus demonstrated when He washed the feet of His disciples (John 13). Service is the function of the Holy Spirit, who comes alongside to help us and serve us. When a church has a culture of service, people come alongside the pastor and leadership team to serve in whatever capacity is needed. My advice to people looking for an area to volunteer is to "just pick up the towel and serve." Eventually they find a niche that works for them and the betterment of the church.

Not everyone wants to be a leader, but everyone has within him or her a desire to be part of a team. Volunteers are the "Dream Team" that moves the church forward. Serving in the church provides people with a way to fulfill their God-given calling to help people and build the kingdom of God.

THINGS TO THINK ABOUT

1. What areas are you involved in as a volunteer at your church?

2. What other areas are you interested in?

3. How would you rate yourself in these four categories: *willing*, *on time*, *responsible*, and *kingdom-focused?*

DAY 23

A Bringing Culture
Miracles happen when we bring people to Jesus.

THE "POWER OF BRINGING" is one of the greatest powers on earth. John 1:42 records how Andrew brought his brother to Jesus. Jesus looked at this young fisherman and said, "'Your name is Simon, son of John—but you will be called Cephas' (which means 'Peter')." That day, on the shores of Galilee, Peter met Jesus, and his life was never the same. Over the next few years of following Jesus, Peter experienced extraordinary changes in his character, maturity, and effectiveness. He was transformed from an unstable and often inconsistent businessman into a leader and pillar in the Christian church.

Peter was the first person to preach the message of Christ after the resurrection. He challenged people to respond, and three thousand people made decisions to follow Jesus, thus launching the first church. A few days later, another five thousand were added to the church.

The book of Acts records that on one occasion, Peter went to the town of Joppa in Israel to pray for a woman who had died. She was raised from the dead, and the whole community turned to the Lord. That was just one of many miracles Peter did.

On another occasion, after receiving a vision from God, Peter traveled to the house of Cornelius, a Gentile (non-Jew), to tell him about Jesus. Cornelius and the Gentiles with him believed in Jesus, were filled with the Holy Spirit, and were baptized. This was the first instance of non-Jewish communities receiving the gospel, and it opened the door to the entire world.

Peter even wrote two books that are part of the New Testament: 1 and 2 Peter. His influence continues to serve and instruct believers today.

You and I belong to Christ because the good news went to both the Jewish and Gentile people. We are the result of the power of bringing. Andrew *brought* Peter to Jesus, Peter's life was changed, he became instrumental in *bringing* Jews and Gentiles to Jesus, and today the gospel of Jesus and the Christian church exist on every continent.

There is no way Andrew could have known the calling hidden inside his brother, much less brought about this level of change on his own. Andrew simply brought Peter to Jesus, and Jesus did the rest. That is the *power of bringing*. We are called to bring people to Jesus, to introduce them to the only one who can accomplish true life transformation.

THE POWER OF A BRINGING CULTURE

Over the years I've been in church leadership, I've seen the "power of bringing" on many occasions. A person brings a friend, for example, and a whole household of people come to the knowledge of Christ. I have seen as many as seventy-five people come to Christ through one person who was brought to Jesus.

When a church culture is one of honor, relationship, worship, and generosity, people want to bring their friends. Who wouldn't want to be in an environment like that? We like to tell people, "Everyone needs Jesus, and everyone needs a home. Will you come with me to my church? You're going to love it!"

The prophet Isaiah predicted people would want to take others to meet their God in church. He wrote, "People from many nations will come and say, 'Come, let us go up to the mountain of the Lord, to the house of Jacob's God. There he will teach us his ways, and we will walk in his paths'" (Isaiah 2:3).

OVERCOMING BARRIERS TO THE BRINGING CULTURE

In Mark 2 there is a story about four men who brought a paralyzed friend to Jesus. They had to break through several "barriers to bringing" in order to get the man to Jesus.

Barrier 1: The fear of failure or rejection

What if the person you intend to bring does not respond to your invitation? The answer is simple. God has inspired you to give the invitation, and He is simply asking for your obedience. The results are up to Him. The only failure would be refusing to obey. It may take many invitations over the course of a person's life before he or she accepts. Sometimes the fruit is not seen for many years.

Barrier 2: The weight of responsibility

The four friends had to carry the man to Jesus. That couldn't have been easy, especially when they discovered they were going to have to somehow get him up on the roof. We are called to help lift people who are limited in their strength. Galatians 6:2 says, "Carry each other's burdens, and in this way you will fulfill the law of Christ" (NIV).

Barrier 3: The inconvenience of the process

When they got to the house where Jesus was, they discovered the house was full. This didn't stop them, though. They climbed onto the roof, tore away some tiles, and let the man down in front of Jesus. *Bringing* is more than just *inviting*. It might mean finding creative solutions to obstacles people face when it comes to attending church. It might mean going out of your way to pick them up or riding with them on the bus.

Ultimately the paralyzed man received not only physical healing but also forgiveness for his sins. He walked away totally restored. Break through the barriers and join the bringing culture. You might change not only one person's life but generations to come. Lives will be saved and the influence of your own life multiplied.

THINGS TO THINK ABOUT

1. Who brought you to Jesus? How has your life changed since then?

2. Write down the names of three or four people you could bring to church.

3. What are the barriers to bringing people to Jesus that most hold you back?

Amber's Story

I grew up with fighting, abuse, hatred, divorce, and selfishness being the norm. In elementary school I was awkward and shy, and I was bullied for it. When I hit middle school, things started to really go downhill. I was constantly at war with myself and others. I struggled with feeling purposeless, hopeless, and depressed. My relationships with my friends and family were nothing but destructive.

Slowly my friendships started to disintegrate until I got to a place where I was nothing but lonely. I lived with this constant question playing in the back of my head: "Why am I here? Is there even a point in living?" It was in middle school that I first attempted to commit suicide. I had finally cracked. I had reached such a low, desperate state that I thought this kind of life wasn't worth living any longer.

Jump a couple of years to high school, and things weren't looking any better. I was still living in a constant state of depression, replaying that same question in my head: "Why am I here?"

One day, in English class, I met Jade. She was the first person to invite me to church. When she initially asked me to come, I rejected her right away. I had a very negative view of church and was not prepared to go. Eventually, after a month of Jade continually inviting me, I decided to go.

The moment I walked into the building, I was hit with a huge sense of family and community, which was something I had never really felt before. Everyone was friendly, inviting, and genuinely happy to see me there. I was shocked by the overwhelming love I felt.

Not long after coming to Home Church Youth, I gave my life to Jesus, and at that moment everything changed. For the first time in my life, I felt loved, wanted, accepted, and purposeful. For the majority of my life, I hadn't been sure what I was living for. I was simply existing. But when I met Jesus and got saved, I knew there was a bigger calling on my life. I had some major issues I had to deal with that were affecting my day-to-day life, but once I was free from my rejection, abuse, self-hatred, and abandonment, I felt for the first time like I was actually living.

There was—and still is—this burning desire to tell others about what happened to me as a result of finding my Savior, Jesus. I couldn't live life knowing there were so many others who don't know this love, including my brother, who was going through the same thing I was. After several months of convincing and begging my brother, he finally came to church with me. It wasn't long before he got radically saved, just as I did, and now he is bringing other people to Jesus as well.

One girl—Jade—was persistent about sharing Jesus, and a ripple effect started that led to many others getting saved. Her obedience led to the salvation of many, and that is why I bring people to Jesus.

DAY 24

A Life-Giving Culture
*The church is a place where life is communicated
in both what is said and done.*

CHANTELLE CAME TO our church for the first time in 2011. She
had arrived in Canada from another country and was looking
for a church that would meet her needs and help her grow
spiritually.

She entered the church cautiously, wondering what kind of
church this was and how she would be received. I introduced
myself to her with a smile and welcomed her to our church.
When she discovered I was the pastor, she immediately asked
me a pointed question: "Pastor, is this a church that condemns
people?"

I was surprised by her question, since that's not usually the
first thing a guest asks. "No," I replied. "We welcome and love
people. Why do you ask?"

Chantelle began to tell me about her past church experience.
In her country she had attended several churches that were
strongly condemning toward people. She told me the pastor of
her church often spoke in his messages about specific sins people had committed, and sometimes he even referred to people
by name. She made it clear that if we were a church that condemns and criticizes its people, she would not be back. "I'm just
here to check you out," she said.

I wasn't offended by her bluntness. I was sad her church
experience had been so different than the gospel of grace, acceptance, and love Jesus preached. I assured her that we were

not a condemning church but rather a life-giving one and that I was committed to preaching faith-filled, edifying, encouraging messages.

Jesus is the model life-giver. Life was a common theme in His teachings. He said, "I have come that they may have life, and that they may have it more abundantly" (John 10:10 NKJV). On another occasion he said, "The very words I have spoken to you are spirit and life" (John 6:63). And later, "I am the way, the truth, and the life" (John 14:6). Jesus came to give us life. If giving life was His goal, shouldn't it be ours as well?

DON'T THROW ROCKS

Unfortunately, Chantelle's experience in church is all too common. Many people come from legalistic backgrounds that are negative in their approach to the Christian message. These church cultures see Christianity only as a set of rules, of dos and don'ts, of principles to be obeyed rather than life-giving truths that bring freedom. They see God as a strict disciplinarian in the sky who is always looking for a reason to punish His people, rather than a God of grace who is there to help and forgive in time of need.

Christianity is not about obeying rules. It is about a relationship with God, a lifestyle of grace, and an internal power to live transformed lives. Jesus made it clear that through Him our hearts are changed and we are set free to conquer sin, addiction, and temptation. Jesus' internal work in our hearts is far more effective than external rules and regulations set up by religion.

God is not a legalistic God but rather a God of faith, hope, and love. Jesus came to establish the New Covenant, which means a new way of relating to God—a relationship based on *forgiveness* through Jesus, empowered by the *resurrection* of Jesus, and characterized by the *grace* of Jesus.

The religion of Jesus' day was a religion of condemnation.

One day the religious leaders brought to Jesus a woman who had been caught in adultery. They told Him of her sin and wanted Him to approve stoning her to death. In other words, they wanted Him to join their negative, condemning approach toward sinners.

Jesus refused. Instead He told the woman's accusers, "Let the one who has never sinned throw the first stone!" (John 8:7). Ashamed, the men left, one by one. None of them were perfect, yet they had demanded that the woman be judged for her sins. Can there be a clearer picture of the nature of condemnation? Who are we to accuse and condemn others, since none of us are perfect either?

There was one person present who had never sinned: Jesus. He could have thrown the first stone. But He didn't. He asked the woman, "Where are your accusers? Didn't even one of them condemn you?" (verse 10).

She replied, "No one, Lord."

I can imagine the forgiveness and love in Jesus' eyes as He looked at this broken woman and said, "Neither do I condemn you; go and sin no more" (verse 11).

Jesus was not saying sin is inconsequential. Sin has a devastating effect on our lives. That's why He told her she needed to change. When we truly know Jesus, we find ourselves motivated and empowered from within to live a life of obedience. Instead of striving to achieve impossible perfection, we rest in Jesus' finished work and God's unconditional acceptance of us, while simultaneously embracing the process of change.

Rules demand perfection, but Jesus provides grace and power for the process. Rules restrict, but Jesus sets us free. Rules can never be satisfied, but God is already satisfied because Jesus absolved our sin on the cross. Now we are free to live out our salvation day by day, continually being transformed into God's image. Every day is a chance to be more like Jesus. Yes, we will fail sometimes—but His mercies are new every morning.

Jesus came to give us eternal life, a life that will never end. That includes an abundant life on earth, filled with the blessings of God. I believe with all my heart Jesus wants to help us truly enjoy life, to live life to the fullest. Life with Jesus becomes more and more abundant as we draw closer to Him and discover the freedom He offers.

CULTURE OF LIFE

By definition, a life-giving church culture cannot be a condemning culture, because condemnation is the opposite of the life Jesus brings. Everything in the church must produce life; it must lead people toward the fullness and enjoyment of life.

How do we create a life-giving culture? There is only one way: we must be life-giving people. Culture is the reflection of the people within the culture. Our goal as leaders and members must be to enjoy life ourselves and to inspire life in others

At Home Church we decided long ago to develop a life-giving culture. We want the same life-giving environment in each of our locations around the world. Pastors and leaders, in particular, must be life-givers. They must believe in, value, and facilitate the life of Jesus flourishing in the people.

At the end of every service in every location, our leaders pronounce this blessing on the people: "The Lord bless you and keep you; the Lord make his face shine on you and be gracious to you; the Lord turn His face toward you and give you peace" (Numbers 6:24-26 NIV).

THINK LIFE, SPEAK LIFE

We give life by the words we speak. Our words have the power to condemn or the power to give life. Remember what Proverbs

18:21 says: "The tongue can bring death or life; those who love to talk will reap the consequences." In order to become life-giving people who contribute to a life-giving culture, we must learn to speak life-giving words.

According to James 3:10, blessing and cursing can come out of the same mouth; therefore, we must carefully choose the words we speak. James teaches that our words are like a rudder that steers a ship, a bit that guides a horse, or a forest fire that burns out of control. In other words, our mouths have a lot of power, and we must take care to control what we think and say. We should only speak things that bring positive direction, healing, and blessing.

Our words come from our thoughts. Jesus said, "Whatever is in your heart determines what you say" (Matthew 12:34). A good rule of life is to always choose higher thoughts about people than you know they have for themselves. That way your words will inspire life.

When you think higher thoughts about people, you are agreeing with God. His thoughts about people are always higher than their thoughts about themselves. He said in Isaiah 55:9, "For just as the heavens are higher than the earth, so my ways are higher than your ways and my thoughts higher than your thoughts."

When people are sick, speak words of healing and health. When people are depressed, speak words that lift them up. When people are dysfunctional in their relationships, speak words of unity and blessing. I often tell people, "You will be great and you will be a blessing." Those were God's words to Abraham, and we are children of Abraham, so they are true for us as well!

The words we speak can release blessing, protection, grace, and the favor of God in people's lives. Let's make the most of every opportunity to think life, speak life, and give life everywhere we go.

THINGS TO THINK ABOUT

1. Why are the grace and presence of Jesus more effective than rules and law?

2. Who can you encourage and give life to this week?

Bobby's Story

My path toward a relationship with Jesus started in 1998 while golfing with a friend at the Balmoral Golf Course in Red Deer, Alberta. My friend could hit a 300-yard ball with ease, but I could barely hit a 220-yard ball. On one hole I tried to hit the ball further. I ended up swinging too hard, and I felt something pop in my lower back.

Weeks went by, and I started to feel pain in my back and my left leg. I had an MRI to see what the problem was. I was told I had near total loss of disc height in my L5 S1 vertebrae. I had surgery to repair the sciatic nerve, but my back didn't improve.

I continued in pain for a number of years on various medications and also marijuana. I thought the pot was helping, but I continued using more and more and started losing a lot of weight. I began growing marijuana in my basement and even selling some to pay bills. I looked in the mirror one day and realized that at 130 pounds, I was in serious trouble. Things had gotten out of hand.

That's when I called out to God to help me. I told God, "If you are real, help me get free from this addiction to pot." I fell to my knees. I was at rock bottom.

When I got up, I took a one-pound bag of pot and started flushing it down the toilet. The power to do that must have come from God, because I was so addicted and financially broke I could never have done it on my own.

That was on February 13, 2004. The problem was I still had about seventy pot plants in my basement. The morning of February 14, a knock came at the door. It was a police officer with a document from a previous drug charge. He asked, "Do you have marijuana plants growing here?"

I said, "Yes, I have a few." I was so tired of the way I was living that I wanted to confess.

He went away, but I knew he would come back with a warrant to search my home. The next day the police returned and busted me for marijuana production and trafficking. But they didn't take everything. They left enough for me to start production again. I believe they were setting me up to capture more people.

However, I called a friend from Red Deer to come with a truck to help me get rid of everything pot-related in my basement. We went to the Blackfalds dump with a truckload of pot plants and equipment. Between what I flushed and the trip to the dump, the Lord gave me the strength to get rid of drug paraphernalia worth about nine thousand dollars.

I decided to call my brother-in-law, Rick. I needed guidance, and I knew he was a strong Christian. Rick came by that afternoon. I put it all out there, and he led me in a prayer that radically changed my life in the best way possible. I received Christ into my heart, confessed my sins, and asked for forgiveness.

The next Sunday I went to church for the first time as a new Christian. That day, February 22, 2004, is probably on the list of the ten most memorable days in my life. I sat near the front, next to my brother and his wife. The speaker, named Cindy, said she believed there was someone in attendance with a bad back and pain in their left leg. I was scared because I didn't know many people and I was still detoxing from pot, so I didn't respond. I believed she was talking about me, but I didn't know how she knew about my situation.

After the sermon I was invited to go for prayer, and I agreed. Rick and another person laid hands on my shoulders and prayed in a strange language for me. Something came over me, and I started speaking a language I have never heard before. I was speaking really fast, and then I started laughing uncontrollably and crying at the same time. I didn't know what was going on. I guess the Lord was delivering me. This was all so new to me.

When it all stopped, I had to be helped out of the church, since I could barely walk. My legs were like rubber. We went to Rick's for lunch, but I remember Pastor Mel asking me if I was coming back for the evening service to get baptized, and I said yes. I didn't know what to expect after what had already happened.

We returned for the six o'clock service. Pastor Mel was speaking. After I was baptized, I sat next to Rick again, and Pastor Mel was preaching a message on healing. He mentioned if Jesus is healing you, you may feel heat in the area of your pain. That reminded me of what Cindy said about my back in the morning service.

I wondered why I hadn't acknowledged what she said and received prayer for my back. Maybe I could have been healed. That must have been when my faith to be healed kicked in, because suddenly heat started from the crown of my head down to the problem area of my back. To this day I don't know how to explain it. It was like an electric heat or warm shiver going down my back three times. It was the best feeling I have ever experienced. To me, it was God healing my back. For the next three weeks, I felt the warm shiver go down my back several times a day. I never wanted it to stop. What a work the Lord was doing!

Many miracles happened in my life in February 2004. The doctor had told me I could be paralyzed if I lifted anything heavier than a coffee pot. However, Rick asked me to come work for him at his bottled water company. I told him I believed the Lord had healed my back and that yes, I would. For the next two years, I hauled five-gallon water jugs around Red Deer with no pain or problems with my back or leg.

Those three weeks healed everything. I told the doctor God had healed my back and I would never take pills or pot for my back again. Since then I have been running a company called Most High Siding Ltd.—not because I'm high, but because He is the Most High. He continues to be a blessing in my life, and I still attend Home Church. My roots are planted in Christ.

He is more than sufficient for your needs. He wants a personal relationship with you every day, not just Sunday. Let Him use you to be a blessing to others, just like He used Rick and the church to be a blessing to me. Jesus loves you! God bless, and keep the faith.

LEAD THE WAY

The church that changes the world

DAY 25

Catch the Vision
A church with a vision can bring change to the world.

ONE OF THE business leaders from Home Church was driving down Queen Elizabeth II Highway, the principal highway that connects the major cities of Alberta. Suddenly and unexpectedly, he was overwhelmed with emotion and moved to tears. He had to pull over on the side on the highway.

With tears flowing down his face, he began to see a vision from God of where our church was headed in the future. At the time, we were a church of less than a thousand people in six different locations. He saw a huge globe with hundreds of lights all connected together, like one networking system. He noticed that many of the lights were in the remotest places of the globe.

He understood we would not just be a church with locations in Canada, but we would become a global church with a vision for every nation on earth. The lights represented ever-connected relationships that worked together to bring light and life around the world. He saw leaders trained, pastors raised up, church locations formed, and people equipped to do the work of the ministry. He saw us growing from a local, Canadian church to a global church.

When he was finally able to settle his emotions, he pulled back on the highway and continued driving. The vision was so strong he couldn't wait to tell me about it. With his eyes still filled with tears, he took the exit toward our church. When he arrived he went straight to my office and shared what he had seen.

His vision was so encouraging to me at that moment. Years earlier, when we were first starting the church, we had received the vision of a wheel with its hub and spokes on fire. Over the years God had done great things through our church. We had been instrumental in planting churches both in Canada and internationally. But I was actually a bit discouraged during that season because we weren't accomplishing everything as quickly as I thought we would. Vision usually takes longer to accomplish than you think, I've discovered; and I had started to wonder if we were truly called to reach the world or if I had dreamed too big.

That encounter with God sparked even greater faith in all of us for the days ahead. It confirmed what we already had believed: that our church was called to reach some of the darkest, most remote places on the planet.

Today that vision is being fulfilled, although there remains more to do. Our church is in many continents and in some of the most unreached places on earth, including places of great persecution and danger.

VISION DEFINED

A vision is something you *see* that moves you to *action*. The Old Testament prophet Zechariah was just a sleepy prophet until an angel woke him up with a vision. The angel asked him, "What do you see?" (Zechariah 4:1 NKJV).

Zechariah began to describe what he saw: olive trees, golden pipes, and a golden lamp. He didn't understand what God was saying, so the angel gave him this prophetic message:

> "Not by might nor by power, but by My Spirit,"
> Says the Lord of hosts.
> "Who are you, O great mountain?

> Before Zerubbabel you shall become a plain!
> And he shall bring forth the capstone
> With shouts of "Grace, grace to it!"
> (verses 6-7 NKJV)

Another prophet, Haggai, joined Zechariah. Together their visions from God inspired the people of Israel to restart repairs on the temple of God, something that had been delayed by opposition from Israel's enemies (Ezra 5, Haggai 1-3). When a vision is caught, it moves you to action. Often it becomes a passion that captivates your heart. Church leadership must have a clear vision from God, not just go through the motions of religious duty without true purpose. Likewise, church members should catch the vision of the house and use their talents and time to help accomplish it.

NOW WHAT?

Once you receive a vision from God, how do you respond? What do you do next?

The prophet Habakkuk was depressed about the injustice in the world, and he started asking God some very direct questions. As part of His answer, God told Habakkuk, "Look around at the nations; look and be amazed! For I am doing something in your own day, something you wouldn't believe even if someone told you about it" (Habakkuk 1:5). God wanted Habakkuk to look into the future and see that things would not always remain the same. God had great plans, and He would make sure they were carried out.

Habakkuk received a vision, but he didn't know how to respond. A few verses later, God told Habakkuk what he should do with the vision. He said:

Write the vision
And make it plain on tablets,
That he may run who reads it.
For the vision is yet for an appointed time;
But at the end it will speak, and it will not lie.
Though it tarries, wait for it;
Because it will surely come,
It will not tarry.
(2:2-3 NKJV)

God's exhortation to Habakkuk gives us five keys to responding properly to God's revealed vision in our lives. As active participants in the kingdom of God, especially within the context of our local churches, these keys will help us fulfill God's calling and walk into the future He has for us.

1. Write the vision.

Vision must be put into words. Clearly stating your vision helps others catch the vision and make it their own. Take time to think, pray, and meditate on the direction God has given you for your life; then write down specific things you believe God has in store. Dream big, but then take the next step of commitment by writing down what you believe God is calling you to become and accomplish.

2. Make it plain.

Vision must be practical. It's not enough to have a vague sense of purpose or destiny. God wants to give us specific steps, strategies, and goals. You should be able to clearly and simply communicate the calling God has for your life and your church.

3. Read it and run with it.

Running implies urgency and excitement. We run when we simply can't wait to be somewhere or do something. God's vision should excite and motivate us. Once we catch His vision, we will find ourselves expending energy and investing resources wholeheartedly because we are consumed with a calling.

I often tell Heather, "I'm not just walking with the vision, I'm running with it." In recent years, I've actually been *flying* with it—I spend far more time in airports and airplanes than most people my age, and I love it! The vision of God's church established throughout the earth wakes me up in the morning and fills my dreams at night.

4. Wait for it.

God's vision often seems to be delayed. In those moments the vision is tested, and so is our faith as leaders. God's timing is always perfect, however; and if we faithfully wait for His vision, it will come to pass.

5. Faith it.

Don't fake it—faith it. Take steps of faith, no matter how small, in the direction of the vision. When your emotions, circumstances, or lack of resources seem to contradict the vision, allow your faith to lead your decisions. Remember the vision, speak the vision, pray for the vision, and believe the vision. God's plans always come to pass, and sooner or later you will see the reward for your faith.

VISIONS, LEADERS, AND TEAMS

I often tell people we are a *vision-driven, leadership-led, team-built church*. Each of those three adjectives is important.

1. Vision-driven

The first vision God gave us, the wheel on fire, occurred before we had officially launched the church. I was only twenty-five years old at the time. Thirty-seven years later, the Holy Spirit spoke clearly to me that we were to take the multi-site vision to the nations. God's vision was to branch a church in every nation on earth. Today we conduct regular online staff meetings with leaders all around the world who give oversight to our church locations.

God is the originator and giver of the vision. The vision does not originate with a group of leaders or a board, and we can't take credit for it. It is God's vision. We are simply recipients, called by God to take steps of faith and obedience to accomplish what He said He would do.

When God gives a vision, He chooses individuals to fulfill the vision. God called Moses to deliver Israel from Egypt and lead the nation to the Promised Land. Jesus called Peter to launch the church on the day of Pentecost and later to open the door of faith to the Gentiles. Saul had an encounter with God on the road to Damascus, then he received a prophetic vision from Ananias, and eventually he became the world-changing apostolic leader and New Testament writer we know as Paul.

When God calls you, He gives you a task, and He promises to be with you all the way. God always has a man or woman to fulfill His vision.

2. Leadership-led

God's vision directs and drives the church, but He sets leaders in place to help guide the day-to-day activities and advancement toward His vision. The Bible often uses the terms *pastor* or *elder* to describe the men and women who lead the church.

The church is not a democracy or a monarchy but a theocracy, which means God is in charge. He said, "I will build my church, and the gates of Hades will not overcome it" (Matthew 16:18 NIV). Pastors are under-shepherds, serving under the oversight and authority of the Chief Shepherd, Jesus. Peter wrote to the elders in the churches:

> Care for the flock that God has entrusted to you. Watch over it willingly, not grudgingly—not for what you will get out of it, but because you are eager to serve God. Don't lord it over the people assigned to your care, but lead them by your own good example. And when the Great Shepherd appears, you will receive a crown of never-ending glory and honor.
> (1 Peter 5:2-4)

Leaders must give account to God for their actions. That means leaders should take their calling seriously, and those under their care should respect their leadership as a God-ordained benefit in their lives. The Bible says, "Obey your spiritual leaders, and do what they say. Their work is to watch over your souls, and they are accountable to God" (Hebrews 13:17).

Leaders often ask me what the role of the board should be in fulfilling the vision. I reply by explaining what a vision-driven, leadership-led, team-built church means. The board's calling is to serve the vision of the house. The board does not set the direction for the church and its ministries; the board guides the vision and ensures everything is handled legally and with financial integrity. I am so thankful for faithful board members who have exemplified an attitude of service to the vision of the house in unity and honor. This has been an essential part of seeing the vision fulfilled.

3. Team-built

After God calls a man or women to lead, it is the leader's responsibility to form a team. Moses formed a team of twelve leaders of Israel, and he later expanded the team to include leaders of thousands, hundreds, and tens. Peter had a team of eleven other apostles. Paul built a great team of leaders; some of them accompanied him on his travels, and others remained in the different cities he visited, raising up churches and other teams.

Leaders are responsible to share God's vision with their team. Then the team works together to develop strategies, do the work, and fulfill the vision. The real success of a church is the development of a team that can work together for the advancement of the good news.

I'll never forget the day I shared with our leaders that our church would someday be in one hundred different international locations. My announcement shocked the leaders and the people present; however, they believed the vision, and together we began working as a team to accomplish it.

I remember when Brian Thomson came to my office and shared with me that God had called him to build homes for orphans in Africa and feed hungry children. His vision was impossible by human standards, but we both knew God had called him. Today the Home of Hope vision is thriving, with a team of great leaders and volunteers who are extending the kingdom of God and aiding thousands of children. Only God Himself could have established the work, and He did it through leaders who were faithful to believe the vision and form a team.

Team ministry is one of the most exciting, fulfilling aspects of church life. Without a team that understands and wholeheartedly embraces the vision, the vision will not come to pass. Leaders need to be intentional about raising up new leaders and teams, especially in younger generations. The church and the vision should outlast the leader, but this will only happen if healthy teams are formed and released to do the work of the ministry.

THE CHURCH I SEE

Your vision will move you toward your destination. What kind of church do you see? What role do you see yourself fulfilling in the church? What is your level of faith regarding the vision? What can you do right now to move toward the future God has for you? The answers to those questions will determine whether you move toward the future or remain where you are.

I've spent my life studying what the Bible says about the church as well as building the church. Let me tell you about the church I see, in the hopes it will inspire you to a greater vision for your own life and involvement.

The church I see is a multi-site, international church with the same beliefs, values, culture, and flow of life in every location. It is one church in many locations.

The church I see is both local and global. It focuses on reaching its local community with the good news of Jesus, but it has a strategy to branch into other regions and other nations of the world.

The church I see is bigger, better, and greater. *Bigger* means it continually reaches more people for Christ; *better* means it continually builds leaders and people; and *greater* means it continually increases its influence in the world.

The church I see fulfills the great commission: preach the gospel, make disciples of nations, change the world.

The church I see is a church without limits. It is a church that can grow and expand indefinitely. It is an equipping church where lost people are saved, disciples become leaders equipped to serve, and people are raised up to impact their world.

Can you catch the vision of God's church in the earth? Do you want to be part of the cause of extending the good news of Jesus through a great, global church? People with this kind of vision can change the world.

Always remember: "What you see is what you will be." What can you see?

THINGS TO THINK ABOUT

1. What does the word "vision" mean to you?

2. What do you think God's vision for your life is?

3. How can you help fulfill the vision of the church where God has planted you?

Craig's Story

My faith journey began at an early age. I was born the second child in an Irish Catholic family. We were educated through the Catholic school system and only nominally practiced our faith. My father believed in God, but due to his own trauma, he lived a life where alcohol was the main method to subdue his pain. He succumbed to his addiction and died when I was thirteen years old.

Needless to say, this had a dramatic effect on my life. As a teen I lived a destructive lifestyle that included drugs, violence, and alcohol. I was an angry young man who was always searching, asking questions, and exploring the meaning of life. These questions led me to start practicing Transcendental Meditation and embracing the tenants of Maharishi Mahesh Yogi, an Indian guru. These teachings settled my spirit but didn't meet my spiritual needs.

God was still working on me. It wasn't until after I was married that a friend of mine invited me to church and introduced me to the evangelical faith, which changed my life. When I accepted Jesus Christ into my life, my spirit became calm, forgiveness began to work within me, and God began to mold me into the leader He wanted me to be through the Word of God and teaching.

My wife Rita and I, along with our children Patrick and Natalie, began attending Home Church in 1982. My wife and I had been looking for a place to raise our family and serve God. We embraced and practiced the principle of tithing, which included giving our time and service to the church. Our talents are God-given, and therefore we should use them in the church. With that in mind, we presented ourselves to our pastors to work in any area that our individual skill sets would help our local church community.

Over time the church leadership gave us many different tasks, including assuming lead roles in a number of areas. We did this with a glad heart, knowing that whatever time we put into these tasks was God's time, and it was part of our gift to God.

The church at that time was still relatively young, and Pastor Mel was searching for people who wanted to serve the vision of the church and who understood what true servant leadership is. Those were people who didn't need to push their own agendas but would work to implement the Spirit-led vision. Biblical leaders must have hearts to see the vision fulfilled, knowing that when they work to see God's work done, their reward will be in heaven.

Pastor Mel approached me in 1990 about becoming a board member. He talked to me about my skill set and how I could put my talents to use in our local church. We discussed how a biblical leader in a board role works within the legal framework to serve the vision, not to set the direction for the church. These conversations were important to me because they cemented what I always knew to be truth: when you serve a God-given vision and your heart is right, you can do great things for the kingdom of God.

The board at Home Church embraces this concept. Any person whose name is brought forward goes through a mentorship process where they attend board meetings and learn the role of a modern-day, biblical board member and how an effective board operates. As board members, it is incumbent upon us to serve the vision by ensuring that everything we do complies with all legal and financial regulations. It is also important that we speak our minds to help guide the pastoral team without dictating to them or governing them. We serve the vision with integrity and understanding, and we measure every decision against the Word of God; so it is not blind trust but rather the spiritual function of servant leadership.

DAY 26

Take the Lead
To become a leader, you must step up, step out, and step into God's plan.

MY STORY OF leadership began when I was nineteen years old. It was mid-term during my first year at Bible college. One day the college president approached me and said, "Mel, I have an opportunity for you to consider."

I said, "Yes sir, what is that?"

He replied, "Would you be willing to take the leadership of a small community church for the summer before returning to your second year of college? It's in the town of Minnedosa, Manitoba."

That was the last thing I expected him to say. I hadn't even finished my first year of studies yet. How could I consider preaching several times every week and pastoring people at an actual church? Besides, all I knew of Minnedosa was that it was a tiny town halfway across Canada. This wouldn't exactly be a great financial or career opportunity, that was for certain.

I said, "Sir, what would my responsibilities be?"

He took a deep breath. "The pastor is taking a six-month leave of absence, and you would be pastor for the summer. That means teaching the adult Bible class on Sunday mornings, leading and preaching at the Sunday morning and evening services, and conducting a midweek prayer and Bible study. In addition, you would pastor the people during the week. And if you'd like to, you could start a youth group, since the church currently has no youth ministry."

Now I was really shocked. The thought of speaking four

times a week, plus starting a youth ministry, was overwhelming. I informed the president that I had no speaking experience, I had never presented a message, and in my mind, I did not have the skills or training to do this work.

He already knew all that, of course, so my reasoning didn't surprise him. He said, "That's okay. I'll give you my best sermons and show you how to present them."

I asked him if he had approached others with this opportunity, and he told me he had already talked to both the third-year and second-year students, and no one was willing or able to take on this opportunity. I was his first pick from the first-year class. In other words, he was getting desperate.

He then explained I would live in the back rooms of the church. I would cook for myself on a wood stove. There was no running water, so I would need to bring in water in pails from outside. And the bathroom, needless to say, was far from modern standards. I would have a salary of ninety dollars a month. If I wanted to, I could supplement my salary by working in a nearby honey business three days a week, leaving the rest of the week for church duties.

"When do you need an answer?" I asked him

"Tomorrow morning." And he left me, a bit stunned, to think it over.

I had no idea what to do, but I knew I wanted to do God's will, whatever that entailed. That evening, while others in the dormitory were laughing and talking, I went to my room and knelt down beside a steamy radiator to pray. It was the middle of winter in Canada. I remember asking God, "Is it your will that I go to Minnedosa and take on this responsibility?"

I didn't hear God say anything. The only sound was the *psst, psst, psst* of the radiator.

So I did the next best thing: I decided to ask my mother. I pulled on my warm coat, walked down the street to the nearest pay phone, inserted coins, and called my mom.

After explaining the president's offer, I asked her, "What do you think I should do?"

She replied, "When you were in the womb, I laid hands on my stomach, prayed for you, and dedicated you to the ministry. Son, *go*." Instantly I knew God was answering me. I felt in my heart I was commissioned by God to "go" and do what seemed far beyond my capabilities.

That was how my leadership began, and it has continued to this day. One opportunity led to another, then to another, and then to another.

I wasn't very qualified for that first leadership role, but God's grace was with me. I quickly improved in every area, and I ended up being surprisingly successful there. I cannot emphasize enough how this first step was the most important leadership step in my life. Without it, I would not be the leader I am today.

STEP UP, STEP OUT, STEP INTO

God often develops our leadership when we take steps that seem beyond our capabilities. Many people fail in their leadership because they do not step forward to take the opportunities offered them. Often they do not want to take the lead because they do not want the responsibility that comes with leadership.

To become a leader, you must *step up, step out,* and *step into* the plan of God for your life.

Step up

"Stepping up" means leaving the normal behind. Often this includes some of your friends and other relationships. In fact, when you step up, some of the people you associate with might be the ones who most resist your steps forward, because your advance makes them uncomfortable or insecure. Stepping up means finding a new level of influence, and that influence will often connect you with a new set of people who will become your friends forever.

Step out

"Stepping out" means going where you have never gone before. To experience the miracle of walking on water, Peter had to step out of the boat. Stepping out is an act of faith in response to God's grace.

Step into

"Stepping into" means embracing the calling and plan God has for your life. It means walking into the future, directed and empowered by God, regardless of where God leads.

After three and a half years of training, Peter faced a crucial moment of decision in his leadership development. It was after Jesus' resurrection and ascension. A group of 120 people, including the disciples, were praying in a room when suddenly the Holy Spirit came upon them all. It was obvious God wanted to do something new and powerful, and Peter was the clear choice to take the lead.

First, he *stepped up* to lead the disciples and other followers of Jesus in the room. Then, he *stepped out* and addressed the crowd that had gathered outside, curious about what this new move of God was. As a result of his message, three thousand people were saved, and Peter *stepped into* the new role God had for him as a leader in the newly founded church.

On a much smaller scale, that was what happened to me at nineteen years of age. I *stepped out* of my comfort zone and my peer group, *stepped up* to a level of responsibility and influence beyond my natural ability, and *stepped into* the call of God on my life. I had no idea at the time, but that little church in Minnedosa, Manitoba was the first step of an exhilarating and fulfilling leadership journey.

GOD AND THE LEADER

Over the years, I've seen God call many individuals to fulfill specific purposes. I often say, "God calls a person, God equips a person, and God sends a person." Let's take a look at these three aspects of God's leadership development in more detail.

1. God calls.

Every leader must know the call of God for his or her life. For Moses, it was the moment when God spoke to him from a burning bush and told him He would deliver the children of Israel from Egypt and take them to the land of promise.

God's call isn't always so dramatic, and often it is revealed one piece at a time. But His call is real, and as a follower of Jesus and a leader in His house, you should continually be in the process of discovering and following His will. The Holy Spirit will call you and confirm your calling.

2. God equips.

Moses' equipping started long before the revelation of his call. He spent forty years being trained in Pharaoh's court, followed by forty years hiding in the wilderness. During these years he learned the skills he would need to lead the children of Israel out of Egypt, through the desert, and into the Promised Land. God uses the natural tools of education, training, and experience to prepare you for what He wants you to do.

3. God sends.

God has a unique plan for your leadership life, and He will send you out to fulfill His purpose in your life. You probably won't feel ready—and in your own strength, you're not. You will go in the power, grace, and wisdom of the Holy Spirit. If God has called you, He will be faithful to carry you through to the end and give you success.

THE PATH TO CONQUER

Over the years I have noticed two primary reasons people don't take leadership: fear and unwillingness.

Judges 4 tells the story of an Israelite prophetess named Deborah. At the time, Israel was facing an impossibly strong enemy. God directed Deborah to call Barak, an Israelite leader, to lead the resistance against the enemy army.

Barak agreed—but only if Deborah would go with him. Seeing his lack of faith and strength, Deborah prophesied that the enemy leader would be captured not by Barak, but by a woman. That is exactly what happened. A woman named Jael struck the fatal blow and ultimately sealed the victory.

Deborah and Jael went down in history as true heroes of faith. Barak, on the other hand, is more often remembered for his hesitancy to step up when Israel needed him the most.

Fear and an unwillingness to step out and "take the lead" are some of the greatest hindrances to leadership. Everyone wants to be on the team, but few are willing to assume the risk and responsibility of leadership.

HOW CAN WE BECOME THE LEADERS WE ARE CALLED TO BE?

1. *Courage*

It takes courage to be a leader. When Joshua assumed leadership of Israel from Moses, God told the new leader, "Be strong and very courageous" (Joshua 1:7). When David transitioned the throne to his son Solomon, he told the new king, "Take courage and be a man" (1 Kings 2:2).

Centuries later a young leader named Timothy was leading the great church of Ephesus. He faced doctrinal division and leadership challenges. He received a letter from the apostle Paul saying, "For God has not given us a spirit of fear and timidity, but of power, love, and self-discipline" (2 Timothy 1:7).

"Do not be afraid" were the words of Jesus to His disciples (Matthew 10:31). "Do not be afraid" were the words of Isaiah to the people of Israel (Isaiah 43:1). And "do not be afraid" are the words you must hear in your spirit today if you are to be the leader God has called you to be.

True leaders are able to generate courage when there is no one to give them courage. One day King David and his men returned from battle to find their homes burned, their families kidnapped, and all their possessions stolen. David's men were so distraught that they threatened to kill him; but the Bible says, "David found strength in the Lord his God" (1 Samuel 30:6).

The word "courage" comes from the Latin word *cor*, which means heart. Your heart is the core of your being. It represents your life, your vitality, your passion, your energy. Everything comes out of your heart. Jesus said, "What you say flows from what is in your heart" (Luke 6:45). If you lose your heart, you lose your life. God wants to fill your heart and life with his courage so you can rise above life's circumstances and be the leader God has called you to be.

2. Confidence

Confidence is the inner strength that enables you to assume God-given leadership. Confidence grows out of courage. When you take courage, you gain confidence in God, His promises, and your own ability.

You must take hold of confidence and never let it slip away. Confidence is essential to deal with the circumstances and battles of life. Every opportunity is accompanied by its own set of challenges, and you will need to face those challenges with confidence.

Hebrews 10:35 says, "So do not throw away your confidence; it will be richly rewarded" (NIV). This passage is talking about the confidence that comes from knowing that God's plan will come to pass. When you face challenges, it's all too easy to throw away your confidence and, as a result, miss the opportunities in your path. But if you hold fast to your confidence, you will see the reward and the result.

3. Creativity

As you take courage and build your confidence in God and in yourself, a supernatural power begins to work in you: the power of creativity. Creativity is the force that operated when God looked at an empty mud hole and said, "Let there be light," and suddenly the lights turned on, and in six days a world was created (Genesis 1, 2).

God-given creativity will give you the answers to every problem. There is no challenge you will face as a leader that does not have a solution. Anything is possible when His creativity begins to work in you.

4. Conquer

When courage, confidence, and creativity align in your life, you will have the power to conquer every difficulty you face. The power of leadership is a conquering power. The apostle Paul called us "more than conquerors" through Christ who lives within us (Romans 8:37 NIV). Conquering power means you cannot be defeated: there is always a win and a victory in your future.

THINGS TO THINK ABOUT

On a scale of 1 to 10, score yourself in the following areas:

Courage   (   )
Confidence   (   )
Creativity   (   )
Conquering   (   )

Ask a leader you follow to score you in the same areas.

Courage   (   )
Confidence   (   )
Creativity   (   )
Conquering   (   )

Victoria's Story

Over the past thirty years, my life has been intertwined with the ancient Silk Road that Marco Polo traveled seven hundred years ago. I have had the privilege of impacting many lives for the Gospel, training national leaders, and branching churches in this exotic and strategic part of the world.

How has this been possible? I am not from an influential family, nor am I well-educated or famous. I am just an "insignificant" farm girl from a small town in Central Alberta. I believe there are two keys to the success God has allowed in my life: I was simply obedient to God's call, and I dedicated my life to be a part of the local church where God planted me forty-five years ago.

In the fall of 1974, I was beginning my last year of high school in a small Alberta city. I had been raised in a Christian home and had accepted Christ at a young age, but that summer, I had encountered God in a new way. I was now looking for a church where I could connect and develop relationships. I had no idea God was about to set me on a course for the rest of my life when I joined a group of vibrant young people who were meeting in a hall and called themselves the "People's Church." Mel and Heather Mullen were the pastors of this group in Red Deer, and they had started an outreach in the small city where I lived. That is where my amazing journey began.

At first it wasn't anything spectacular. I learned to be committed in my personal relationship with God and to the local church. I was mentored, trained, and given small responsibilities where I tried my best to be faithful.

Then, in the spring of 1982, I heard an announcement about two mission trips that were being planned for the summer. One team was going to Mexico and the other to Taiwan. I decided I wanted to go to Mexico, as I had no interest in Taiwan or Asia. Soon after, though, the Mexico team was canceled. Even then, I didn't want to go to Taiwan.

But one Sunday, as I sat in the church service, I felt God tell me He wanted me to go on the Taiwan team. I had a little conversation with Him right there in church. I told Him I would agree to go to Taiwan on two conditions. First, I needed the money to go; and second, I had just started a new job and would need the time off. The next day I went to my boss, and he agreed to give me the summer off. Then God miraculously provided the money for me to go. I was on my way!

When our team of fourteen arrived in Taiwan, I was in culture shock! The heat and humidity, the unpleasant smells, the loud and obnoxious sounds, the strange food, the people speaking a language I could not understand—it all proved too much for me, and I began to count the days before I could return to Canada. However, after a couple of weeks of going door-to-door in tribal villages sharing the Gospel, performing street dramas, and praying with complete strangers (via interpreters) to receive Jesus, I began to fall in love with Taiwan.

Upon my return to Canada, I prayed about how I could go back and serve for a longer period of time. After three years I had the opportunity to return for a six-month period and work with students on a university campus.

During this time I felt God speak to me about mainland China and the unreached people groups there. I had the opportunity to visit northwest China in 1986, and I moved there in 1988 to study Chinese and teach English. Of course, my main purpose for being there was to share the Gospel; and during my five years in that remote city, I was able to disciple several small groups of believers and see over forty people baptized in bathtubs! We had to do everything secretly, as it was illegal to convert the local citizens to Christianity.

In the early nineties, I began to hear about how Communism had fallen across the border in Central Asia and how the indigenous people groups there were opening up to the gospel. At that time there were only a handful of believers among the Central Asian Muslim people groups. In 1993, with counsel from Pastor Mel Mullen and my church in Canada, I made the move to Central Asia. I joined with a local Russian-speaking church there that was growing and planting churches all over the region. Over the thirteen years I lived in that region, I had the opportunity to branch a church among a previously unreached ethnic people group as well as direct a training center to train nationals and send them out to surrounding nations.

Then, in 2006, I began to feel a change was coming in my life, but I couldn't get a clear word from God about what that change would be. One day, over lunch with Pastor Heather Mullen, God dropped the word "Istanbul" into our conversation. By the end of the lunch, it was confirmed: we both felt strongly that I should move to Istanbul and branch Word of Life (which would later become Home Church) in this strategic hub city which connects Europe and Asia. It has now been over ten years since I moved to Istanbul with a team from Central Asia. Today we have a leading church and have just been able to purchase a miracle facility in this great cosmopolitan city. I serve as the overseeing pastor for Home Church EuroAsia. We have several other locations in Central Asia and Europe.

As I look back over my life, I am so thankful that when I was still a young teenage girl, God in His amazing foreknowledge placed me in Home Church with Pastors Mel and Heather Mullen. He had great plans for my life and knew they would only be fulfilled within the context of the local church. I am a part of the great global vision of Home Church to branch churches into every nation on earth, and I am confident we will see God do amazing things along the Silk Road in the coming years!

DAY 27

Swivel Leadership
Leaders pass on their experience and truth to others.

A FEW YEARS ago, my son Jachin was teaching at a leadership meeting with our staff. He began to talk about the idea of "swivel leadership," a concept Pastor Kevin Gerald had shared with him. It's a simple but powerful way to visualize the effectiveness of leadership that is passed on to successive generations of leaders.

We've all sat in a swivel chair. Kids are endlessly entertained by these chairs, of course, and usually end up dizzy or on the floor. But the main purpose of a swivel chair is to give the person seated the ability to be facing one way and then spin around and face the other way.

Jachin used the simple analogy of a swivel chair to describe how good leaders pass on what they learn to others. Leaders gather their teams to teach, train, and impart a truth, direction, or vision with the expectation that the team members will then take that message and swivel it to their own teams. The process is a never-ending cycle of giving and receiving.

What we receive is never just for ourselves—it is always to share with others. There is a mutual submission and humility built into the process, because inevitably teachers learn from students, and leaders learn from followers. Together we become more like Christ and learn to live abundant lives. That is the power of swivel leadership.

Swiveling must have been the process used under the leadership of Moses. Without loudspeakers or any form of mass communication, they were somehow able to convey messages and instructions to several million people. They started with the leaders of the twelve tribes, then the information was passed down through an established leadership structure, including captains of thousands, hundreds, and tens.

You are a leader if you know more than someone else. As a disciple, a follower of Jesus, you learn from the example and training you receive from your leaders. You then swivel your chair toward those who look to you as an example, and you teach them what you have learned. It is as simple as that.

Paul said to Timothy, "You have heard me teach things that have been confirmed by many reliable witnesses. Now teach these truths to other trustworthy people who will be able to pass them on to others" (2 Timothy 2:2). This verse illustrates four successive layers of swivel leadership:

1. Jesus gave Paul revelation and knowledge.
2. Paul swiveled the teaching to Timothy as well as other disciples.
3. Timothy was to swivel what he had learned to trustworthy people.
4. These trustworthy people would then swivel the teaching to other faithful people.

WHAT SHOULD YOU SWIVEL?

1. Swivel what you have experienced.

Your experience is unique and powerful. Tell people the story of your encounter with Jesus: your salvation, your baptism, and all the experiences that have brought you to your present stage of growth.

I love telling the stories of my walk with Jesus: my salvation at age seven, being baptized in the Holy Spirit at eleven, being water baptized in a slimy green creek in Southern Saskatchewan at thirteen, my call to the ministry at seventeen, and other steps I have taken to follow Jesus' calling on my life. Life is a grand adventure, and each of these stories represents amazing moments along the way. Even my struggles, tests, and mistakes have become learning experiences for others to follow.

2. Swivel what you know to be true.

The role of a leader in the church is to pass on God's present message of sound truth to the body of Christ. Each leader adds his or her practical application so the truth is not just theory but practice. This way everyone remains in unity and in the flow of life of the church.

In Home Church, the message is passed from Pastor Jachin, our lead pastor, to Canadian location pastors; meanwhile, on the international level, Brian Thomson and I swivel the message to the leaders of our hub churches around the world. Then they swivel it to the location pastors, who swivel it to leaders of small groups.

3. Swivel unity.

When leaders swivel to the next generation of leaders, the church becomes one and remains one. Sharing what we know with one another creates unity of mind, heart, and spirit.

Becoming one is the key to church health and growth. God's math is "one plus one equals one." That is how marriage works: God took two people in the garden of Eden and made them one. The same holds true in the church. People are added to the church, but the church is still one.

I tried to explain this concept during one church service in our Calgary location. A five-year-old girl sitting in the second row with her mother shouted, "Pastor, you're wrong! One plus one equals *two*."

Everyone laughed, especially me. I said, "Young lady, you're right. But God's math is different than the math they teach in school."

I don't think she believed me. But it's true. With God, 1+1=1 and 100+1=1. That is the power of being one. That is the power of unity.

This kind of unity is unstoppable. When God looked down on the tower of Babel and saw the people were united as one, He said, "nothing they plan to do will be impossible for them" (Genesis 11:14 NIV). Luke wrote that the church in Jerusalem was "of one heart and one soul" (Acts 4:32 NKJV). The apostle Paul told the Philippian church to be "like-minded, having the same love, being one in spirit and of one mind" (Philippians 2:2 NIV).

4. Swivel who you are.

As a leader, you are an example for others to follow. Paul wrote to Timothy, "Be an example to the believers in word, in conduct, in love, in spirit, in faith, in purity" (1 Timothy 4:12 NKJV). Timothy had learned character from Paul; now he needed to swivel that identity toward others by living a lifestyle congruent with godliness. Notice the areas Timothy was to lead by example:

In word

Words are important! What you say and how you say it reflect what is in your heart. Your words show who you really are.

In conduct
Conduct refers to the way we live: how we raise our families, how we relate to our friends, how we operate in business, how we handle decisions, and so on.

In love
Love is the attitude we must display toward others, regardless of who they are, what social status they have, or how they behave. Every person should receive the love Jesus showed: both *agape love*, which is the love of God that we demonstrate to the world, and *brotherly love*, which is the affection we give to others.

In spirit
This refers to the attitudes we have. Attitude affects everything, and our attitudes toward life and toward others make a huge difference in how we lead. We should develop attitudes that reflect godly values, including humility, kindness, faith, courage, and gratitude.

In faith
Faith is believing power. It is trust and confidence in God. It is how we handle the insurmountable problems we face in life. Faith moves mountains and carries us through valleys.

In purity
Purity is choosing to live free from any thoughts, actions, environments, and influences that could lead to a destructive lifestyle.

Paul finished his exhortation to Timothy by saying, "Take heed to yourself and to the doctrine. Continue in them, for in doing this you will save both yourself and those who hear you" (verse 16). In other words, he needed to be an example first in character and action but also in doctrine and teaching.

We have all learned a great deal from our leaders—doctrine, character, morality, and wisdom. When we swivel toward others and demonstrate soundness in those areas of life, we will reproduce who we are. In turn, those people will raise up another generation of leaders, and the church of Jesus Christ will continue to be a blessing to the whole world.

THINGS TO THINK ABOUT

1. Who do you look to for leadership, and what things have you learned from them?

2. Who looks to you for leadership? Who are you swiveling toward?

3. How effective and healthy is your leadership?

4. What are some ways you are an example to others?

My Journey to Lead

By Pastor Jachin Mullen

Growing up, I didn't want to be a lead pastor. Ever. As a matter of fact, when my wife, Becca, and I were dating, she asked me if there was a chance I'd ever be a lead pastor. I said absolutely not. "Good," she replied, "because that would be a deal-breaker."

Yet here we are, more than eight years into our leadership role as lead pastors of Home Church. And we couldn't be happier! What happened to bring us to this point? I'd like to briefly share my leadership journey in the hope it will inspire and encourage you to follow God's plan for your life.

Some of my earliest memories as a child are of my grandparents. Besides my parents, they were the most influential people in my life. They weren't in full-time ministry like my parents, but they were incredible. They had a passion for people and for missions like few people I've ever known.

My mom tells me that when she was a child, she never knew who would be staying over at their house at night. Missionaries from around the world had keys to their home. As a child, I remember sleeping at my grandparents' house and waking up on the couch or floor because a pastor or missionary had come during the night and needed a place to stay. I loved their heart for people and for hospitality.

When I was five or six years old, my grandfather gave me a green cardigan with a capital C on it. I remember him getting down on his knees, putting the cardigan over my head, and telling me, "You're going to be the captain of every team you play on."

Over the years I played hockey, basketball, and other sports. I was never the best player, but I was always the captain. I was good at bringing other people onto the team and leading them to success. I can see now that God was instilling in me a leadership call even as a youth.

However, as a pastor's kid, I also saw the painful side of leadership. I saw the hurt, disappointment, and sacrifice my parents and other pastors experienced from time to time. I decided early on I'd never be a lead pastor. I'd be a great teammate—but not the captain.

As a teenager and young adult, I loved music and youth ministry. I was a youth pastor at age nineteen, and over the next decade I stayed very involved with youth. I led worship, wrote songs, and traveled. Then, when I was about thirty-three, my dad started asking me if I would take the leadership of the Red Deer location. I said no, I wasn't the right person.

My dad kept asking. He's not one to easily take no for an answer. After he had asked me five or six times, I had an honest conversation with him. I told him I wanted a good relationship with him, but I didn't want to be pastor, so could he please find someone else. I thought things were settled after that.

Then early one morning, after Becca and I had been in a season of praying and fasting, something happened that changed me forever. As I swung my feet off the bed and started to sit up, I felt God say in my heart, "The next time he asks, say yes." As I showered and got ready for the day, my mind was suddenly filled with ideas and vision for the church. I began to think about church culture areas that could be adjusted and about strategies to reach Red Deer. How could God change my heart in one second after so many years?

I still had the problem of what to tell my wife, though. After all, I had assured her we would never be lead pastors. Two or three days later, I walked into the kitchen and told Becca what had happened. Even though I felt God had spoken to me, I wasn't going to do this without her agreement. Becca's reply stunned me. She said God had spoken to her three months earlier, and she was ready to go for it.

At this point my dad was respecting my wishes and not pressuring me to lead the Red Deer location. We kept what God had said to us in our hearts and just waited. Over the next few months, we watched as God shifted key areas and people. It was clear he was preparing a way for us to step into leadership.

Then my dad asked again. And this time—hesitantly—I said yes.

I was so scared, to be honest. I thought the church would fall apart under our leadership. My dad is a strong, visionary leader. Once he makes a decision, nothing stops him. But I have a more laid-back personality and leadership style. How was this going to work?

Becca and I decided we needed to simply be who we were made to be. We would do our best to honor the past and honor my parents while listening to what God wanted us to do as leaders. We made some mistakes, of course. When you get excited about leading and vision, sometimes you start changing things without realizing the impact it will have on family dynamics. But my parents were amazing during the transition, and we all worked very hard to maintain unity, obey God, serve the church, and love people.

After we took the lead, the church experienced even more growth than before. We started having ten to fifteen people come to Christ every Sunday. We launched a bus ministry, lunch programs, Christmas outreach programs to the community, and more. We kept the same values as before, but we worked to create a visitor-friendly environment where people could bring their friends.

Eventually my dad asked us to take on the leadership not just of the Red Deer location, but of the entire church. Under our leadership, the church is the same church, but a lot of things have changed. The language we use is different, the aesthetics of the buildings have been modernized, the songs we sing are new. Even the name is new—Home Church. I remember the day I wrote out the phrase, "Everyone needs Jesus. Everyone needs a home." It became our mission and vision statement.

Transitions are never easy, but we all agree that it was worth it. My parents continue to be a key part of the leadership team. Even though our roles have reversed, and even though they are as passionate as ever about the church they've given their lives to for over forty-six years, they have been incredibly humble and generous. They are allowing a new generation to lead. We haven't done everything perfectly, but success isn't about being perfect—it's about having generations of people mutually committed to serving people and moving the church forward. Success is building a strong, healthy, effective team.

Just as a team captain doesn't have to be the best player in every position, so the lead pastor doesn't have to carry the whole church. I don't have to be the superstar. My role is to just build the team. It's to bring people into the roles God has for them, to inspire them to be the best they can be, and to release them to ministry. It's to set people up for greatness. Rather than being intimidated by the success of others on the team, I can celebrate those successes.

Today we are committed to the future and excited about what God is doing in Canada and around the world. I will forever be grateful for my parents and my grandparents because it was their passion for Jesus and for people, their commitment to the church, and their belief in me that brought me to where I am today. But I know the best days are ahead. God is building his church, and each of us has the beautiful privilege of playing a part.

DAY 28

Change Your World
When God's church connects with the world,
everything can change.

WHEN I WAS a child, I remember my mother gathering her five children around a large mixing bowl to make bread. My dad was in a mental institution at the time, and we lived in poverty conditions. We survived on gifts of hand-me-down clothing, food that was dropped off at the door, and mother's delicious home-made bread. I vividly remember "fried doughs," which were pieces of dough that were fried in the frying pan on the old cook stove. It was a special treat every time Mother made bread.

We would crowd around a large mixing bowl, and together we would add flour, eggs, milk, salt, and water. Last of all, we would add yeast to the mixture. I remember the mixture would always begin to bubble as soon as the yeast was added. We would mix it all together with a large spoon, then cover the bowl and set it in a warm place.

As the yeast worked in the mixture, it would take on a new form. After a few hours, my mother would call my two brothers and two sisters and me together around the bowl, and with our little hands we would punch the newly formed dough. Mom would set the huge bowl aside for a while; then she would call us back for another round of punching the dough. Finally, she would cut the dough into pieces, place it in bread pans, and bake it in the oven. The best part, of course, would come a few minutes later, when she would open the oven and we would see a dozen beautiful loaves of bread.

The bread-making experience is one of my fondest memories from childhood. Just as yeast has the power to change whatever it touches, so the church has the power to influence and affect the community around it. When the church touches the community, the community begins to change.

The Bible uses the metaphor of leaven or yeast to describe the influence of the church. Jesus taught His disciples, "The Kingdom of Heaven is like the yeast a woman used in making bread. Even though she put only a little yeast in three measures of flour, it permeated every part of the dough" (Matthew 13:33). In other words, God's kingdom has an invisible but undeniable effect on its surroundings.

The New Testament also frequently uses the metaphor of bread. Jesus is the Bread of Life from heaven (John 6:48–51). Paul wrote that when we participate in the Lord's Supper, we eat "from one loaf of bread," signifying the unity of the church (1 Corinthians 10:13).

Like leaven working in dough, the church is called to impact the community and to bring transformation to the world. Each church in its respective location is called to preach the good news, teach and make disciples, and send its people into their communities and the world with the good news of Jesus and the principles of the Bible. The result will be supernatural change in every sector of society.

SALT AND LIGHT

Leaven and bread weren't the only metaphors Jesus used to illustrate the power of the church to bring change. On another occasion He said, "You are the salt of the earth" (Matthew 5:13).

Why salt? Salt has been used for millennia both to flavor and preserve food. In the same way, churches preserve and enhance their communities. Churches highlight and promote good qualities in neighborhoods, towns, regions, and countries. Just as salt noticeably and unmistakably changes the flavor of the food it seasons, so churches have a clear effect on their communities. There is no mistaking the presence of a healthy, active church in a city. The Message paraphrase renders the verse this way:

> Let me tell you why you are here. You're here to be salt-seasoning that brings out the God-flavors of this earth. If you lose your saltiness, how will people taste godliness? You've lost your usefulness and will end up in the garbage.
> (Matthew 5:13 MSG)

After Jesus called us salt, He used yet another illustration. "You are the light of the world—like a city on a hilltop that cannot be hidden" (Matthew 5:14).

When a light is turned on, darkness has to disappear. When the church is active in its geographical area, reaching and touching every segment of society, the darkness of sin will be abated, and the light of truth will radically and wonderfully transform society.

The church is not to be a fortress or hiding place where Christians retreat to be safe from the world. It is to be a light on a hill. It is to be a center of hope, a source of grace, and a beacon of godliness for those within its reach.

In a previous chapter, I mentioned a mistake I made the first year of Home Church. At the time we were experiencing a great move of God, and many young people were coming to Christ. One day I received a call from a local leader asking me if I would volunteer my time to sit on a counsel to study the needs of young people and help the troubled youth of the city. I informed the person I was too busy meeting the needs of the community to sit on the counsel and give input. I was so church-focused that I didn't include the community in my ministry paradigm.

In retrospect I missed a God-given opportunity for greater influence. He was opening a door for me (and our church) to be a voice and to build a relationship with other people who were genuinely concerned about the community. However, I had never been taught that the church was to be salt, light, and leaven. My view of the church was that it was to be separate and aloof from the world, unaffected and untainted by culture. I did not understand that we could be an influence in the world and yet not be of the world (John 17:12-18).

Today Home Church actively promotes engaging in culture. We seek out and celebrate opportunities to be salt and light in our communities. We encourage people to enter the political arena, to take responsibility in local leadership, and to serve in any place they can be of influence.

Salt is of no value until it is sprinkled from the shaker; darkness is not dispersed until the light is turned on; and cities cannot change until the leaven of the kingdom of God works within them. Each of us needs to ask God how and where to be salt, light, and leaven. How can we make where we live a better place? Who can we serve, love, and assist? What is our sphere of influence, and how can we best reveal Jesus wherever we go? As we make ourselves available for service, every area of our communities will be impacted.

THINGS TO THINK ABOUT

1. Why is it important for the church to become salt, light, and leaven?

2. What are you doing to serve the local community through your church?

3. Besides what your church is doing, are there things you can initiate to be salt and light to the world around you?

4. What changes have you seen in your community as a result of your church becoming salt, light, and leaven?

Bryce's Story

It was August 1993. I was just a few months into being nineteen years old, and life was starting to come apart at the seams. My Die Hard dream of being John McLean running through the Nakatomi Tower saving the world from Hans Gruber and his henchmen was just not going to happen.

I desperately wanted to join the Victoria Police Department, but that dream was slipping away, along with my emotional wellbeing. Depression and anxiety were creeping in, as were some relationships that could potentially take me down a very dysfunctional path. Flat out—I was struggling.

My parents were amazing, and they showed me the grace of God through their patience with me. I attended church regularly; however, in this season, even my faith was an absolute battle. Where was Jesus in all of this? I would find out later He was right there, leading me and guiding me on the right path.

I remember one evening my mom and dad pleading with me desperately, trying to explain the direction my life was heading. Late nights and the bar life were taking a toll on everyone in our family.

In August 1993 they asked me if I would take a trip with them from Victoria to Cowichan River Bible Camp to have a talk with my Uncle Mel, who was visiting with the family from Alberta.

"Uncle Mel? No way!" I responded. He was the last guy I wanted to talk with. He'd probably start preaching at me and telling me I was on my way to hell or something. I knew my uncle was a passionate pastor and his church in Red Deer was pretty upbeat, and I had my concerns.

I reluctantly went with them, hoping to see my cousins and get some family time. If things were executed properly, I figured I could avoid the conversation all together. But, as anyone who knows my uncle could guess, there was no avoiding or skirting the issue. The conversation was going to happen, come hell or high water.

One night after dinner, he said, "Bryce, come join me on the porch. I want to talk with you about your life."

Here we go! *I thought. I remember sauntering out, slumping into the chair, and wondering how I was going to survive the conversation. But surprisingly, Uncle Mel proceeded to ask me questions about my life and be an amazing encouragement to me.*

As we were winding down the conversation, he said, "Bryce, God has an incredible plan for you. It's better than the way you are living right now. He has a ministry for you, a future for you, and life-giving relationships for you. He even has a great girl for you (wink, wink). Don't settle for anything else. He has better! Would you consider coming to Bible school in Red Deer for a semester? You can live in our basement and find this new life."

A new and better life? Move to Red Deer from Victoria? Live in the basement? I listened to his words and thought, He's right...and there are some pretty girls in Red Deer!

I packed up my 1984 Honda Accord hatchback and moved to Red Deer. Uncle Mel very quickly became my pastor. Within a month my relationship with Jesus connected and became more intimate. Pastors Mel and Heather poured discipleship, leadership, and ministry training into my life. Soon I was serving with their son, Pastor Jachin, as his right hand in youth ministry, and life would never be the same.

I look back at that moment on the porch as one of my life's greatest turning points. Since that time, Pastors Mel and Heather have played a huge role in taking me from "the porch to the pulpit." They have trained, coached, prayed, and stood with me through failures and lots of amazing wins. They elevated me from victim to victor, and they empowered me to be the leader God has called me to be. Since the "porch," I have been on the most incredible leadership adventure, including youth pastoring, associate pastoring, and today leading our Home Church loca-

tions in Calgary, Alberta, with my beautiful wife, Glo.

Can you imagine what would happen if we all helped others get past their porch moments by calling out the greatness that is inside of them? I am so glad Pastor Mel saw beyond my present circumstance and showed me the hope, future, and purpose I could not see.

DAY 29

A *Church in Shape*
*Leaders and churches must be strong
in all their values.*

IN A RECENT staff meeting, my son, Pastor Jachin, spoke about the church in balance. He used the example of a pentagon with five equal sides to illustrate five areas of the church that must be equally strong in order for the church to have the correct shape.

Since geometry is not typically part of church staff meetings, we all paid attention to figure out what he meant. First, he drew a series of lopsided pentagons on the board. Some sides were longer, some sides were shorter, and the result was an asymmetrical mess. "These represent a church that is out of shape," he said. "If some areas are emphasized at the expense of others, the church will be unhealthy, lopsided, and misshapen. Is our church in shape? Or do we need to re-shape it?" Turning to the location pastors, he repeated the question. "Is your location out of shape?"

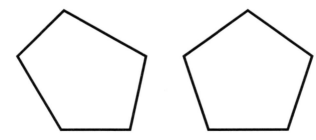

Jachin went on to describe what an out-of-shape church might look like. Maybe a pastor is afraid to speak about giving, so the church doesn't have the resources it needs. Or a church has too few volunteers, and it can't progress because the few who are serving are overwhelmed. Or the weekend services are not well-planned or well-executed, so people don't experience God and learn from His Word the way they should.

He finished by defining the five sides of our church, which I will explain in a moment. As he spoke, I realized that although our church had done well over the years and God had blessed us with great influence, we were a bit out of shape. God wanted to strengthen some areas so we could be the church He was calling us to be.

The phrase "in shape," of course, can have two different meanings. Pastor Jachin first used it to talk about a church with five sides, or emphases, that were of equal importance. But he also used the phrase to talk about a church that is healthy. Just as the human body must be in good condition to maintain proper growth and life, so every church and location needs to be in good condition.

In my travels around the world, I have found that most churches are out of shape. That doesn't mean they are failing— it just means that certain areas are over-emphasized or under-emphasized; therefore, the church is not able to reach its full potential.

For example, a church or location that is strong on relationships but does not teach generosity and giving will usually have difficulty becoming the church God has designed it to be, because of lack of resources. A church or location that only focuses on its weekend services and not on relationships and community might have great worship and preaching, but it will usually struggle in the relational health and care that is required for a growing family of believers.

THE FIVE COMPONENTS OF HOME CHURCH

The shape of the church—both its values and its health—is the responsibility of the pastor and the leadership team. They determine the shape and form God has called the church to take, and they evaluate the condition, progress, and health of the church. Then pastors, leaders, and members work together to adjust the lines where the church is out of shape. As they do, the house of God returns to the shape, health, and functions He designed.

I think the five points Pastor Jachin listed are essential for every church, and any component that is missing or underdeveloped will reduce the church's effectiveness. When each of these components is in balance, however, the church is able to be successful and healthy. Allow me to share the five points with you.

1. *The weekend experience*

This is when the church comes together as one body to worship, grow, and enjoy relationship with one another. You cannot totally experience God's presence in your life without the corporate gathering of His people.

The weekend experience is shaped by four important moments. The first is when the team meets before service, discusses the plans for the day, prays, and sets the atmosphere. The second is when the service begins and people stand and give God their praise. The third is when the message is coming to a conclusion, the pastor gives the call for people to commit their lives to Christ, and people raise their hands to receive Christ. In one glorious moment, they receive eternal life and become children of God. The fourth is when a first-time guest exits the service after connecting with God and other people and says, "I had an amazing experience in church today. I'm coming back next week."

The shape of the church is healthy when the weekend experience is made up of worship, preaching and teaching, giving tithes and offerings, and outreach. Worship is important because it helps people experience the presence of God. Teaching and preaching produce healing, growth, and maturity in people. Giving and outreach challenge people to respond to God's grace and reach out to those around them.

A few years ago, a six-year-old girl named Jaida visited our Calgary location with some friends. Jaida didn't come from a Christian home, but she absolutely loved the church service and her children's classes. She was so excited that she convinced her dad, Peter, to attend church with her. From then on, every week, Peter would sit in the back row of the church while his daughter was in her children's class.

Six months later, after hearing the message of Jesus week after week, Peter raised his hand to receive Christ as his Savior. Immediately and dramatically, his life was changed. His new relationship with Jesus affected his marriage, his attitude, and even his countenance. People started asking his wife, Sandra, "What has happened to Peter?"

Two months after that, Sandra came to a service with Peter and Jaida, and she gave her life to Jesus as well. The entire family is now a key part of our church, and their story is a beautiful example of how God's presence encounters and changes people during the worship experience.

2. Community

Community refers to the relationships between the people of God. The church is to be a vital, vibrant community of believers who practice love toward one another and have wholesome relationships. It is the family of God, a place where people love

one another, encourage one another, and regularly connect with
one another in small groups.

The biblical norm for the church is found in Acts 2, where the
believers met to receive the Word of God both in a public meeting place as well as from house to house. The constant emphasis
not only on weekend services but also on small groups and relationships is vital to keep the house of God in good spiritual shape.

3. Serving

We believe everyone has something to contribute. Being part of
a church family includes having a specific area where you serve.
Serving is not about position or production, it is about finding
a place where you can connect with people and help create a
wholesome, happy church environment. Each week it is vital to
have the right people in the parking lot, at the door, hosting the
service, caring for the children and youth, providing rides to
church, working at the coffee bar, and showing hospitality. Your
act of service helps keep both you and the house of God in the
right spiritual shape.

Serving is essential for the health and wellbeing of the house
of God. The church is in good shape when every person who
attends has a servant heart and has found a place to serve. Paul
put it this way, "Use your freedom to serve one another in love"
(Galatians 5:13).

4. Outreach

Outreach to the local community is an important part of church
life. Our church locations around the world look for ways to
reach out into their communities.

One example of this is the block parties our Canadian churches hold during the summer. We obtain permission from the city to conduct these events in neighborhood parks, and we invite hundreds of neighbors. The block parties are vibrant and exciting, with live music, free food, inflatable bounce houses for kids, games and contests, and a short presentation and invitation to church.

Block parties move Home Church from the building to the neighborhood. The church takes the great love of Jesus to local parks and families, inviting people to discover a relationship with God and with His great church. "Everyone needs Jesus and everyone needs a home" is our message. At block parties we invite everyone to church to meet Jesus and to find a church home.

5. Giving

A church that practices generosity through tithes, offerings, building the church, and giving to the poor is a blessed church. This kind of church has ample provisions to move into the future.

God promises that "The generous will prosper; those who refresh others will themselves be refreshed" (Proverbs 11:25). God is the one who gives seed to the sower, and when that seed is planted in the good soil of God's church, it is multiplied and returned to the sower many times over (2 Corinthians 9:10).

One of our business leaders was struggling financially when he began attending our church. Here's how he describes what happened next.

> I began practicing the principles of tithing and sowing seed. My business began to grow, and today I am in multiple opportunities of international business. I am blessed because of practicing the principles of God and giving, even when at times it took a step of faith to sow a seed. When I sowed that seed, God always provided for my need. I am living in a harvest of blessing that is shaping my future and influence.

THINGS TO THINK ABOUT

1. Weekend service: Do you attend church regularly? What do you most enjoy about the weekly church experience?

2. Community: Do you have close friends at church? Do you attend a small group? How has community contributed to your life?

3. Serving: How are you using your time and talents to help others?

4. Outreach: How are you helping your church reach your community?

5. Giving: Do you give your tithes and offerings regularly? Are you a generous person?

The Most Important Place on Earth
Nothing compares to the house of God.

I TRULY BELIEVE the church Jesus is building today is the greatest and most important place on Earth. This great church was foretold in a prophecy given to Isaiah seven hundred years before Christ.

> In the last days, the mountain of the Lord's house
> will be the highest of all—
> *the most important place on earth.*
> It will be raised above the other hills,
> and people from all over the world will stream there to worship.
> People from many nations will come and say,
> "Come, let us go up to the mountain of the Lord,
> to the house of Jacob's God.
> There he will teach us his ways,
> and we will walk in his paths."
> (Isaiah 2:2-3, emphasis added)

Is there any place on earth that can compare with God's house? Is there any institution or organization on earth that can do what God's church does? The following points are just a few of the benefits of the house of God, particularly as it is expressed in a local church community.

1. In God's house, you can hear the good news, decide to follow Jesus, and receive the gift of eternal life.

A young lady was dealing with a lot of brokenness, trauma, and confusion. Her aunt and a few friends loved her through her pain and gently pointed her toward Jesus. Eventually she attended a Sunday night service in our Red Deer location. She gave her life to Jesus, and her life was dramatically changed.

The change was a process, of course, and the church played a key role in her journey. At church, she found acceptance, love, and a family. As she began to walk into a new life, the community was there to show her the way and help her discover God's purposes for her life. Today she is a healed and whole woman who is committed to helping others find new life in Jesus.

2. In God's house, you can receive spiritual, emotional, and physical healing.

When my wife was in her early thirties, she began to have gallbladder issues. At least once a week, she would suffer through an entire day of intense pain and vomiting. The symptoms progressed to the point where she couldn't even look after our two small children on the days she was sick.

One Sunday at church, as we were having communion, I asked people to form small circles and pray together. Heather had been prayed for many times before, but she believes in being persistent in asking. Everyone in her group joined hands and prayed for her healing.

A week later, she realized she had not had any days of pain. Two weeks went by, and she still had not had any issues. Then a month went by—still no symptoms. After about six months with no pain, she ventured out and tried some of the foods she had not been able to eat at all before. There was no adverse reaction. She had been healed through a simple prayer of faith.

3. In God's house, your mind can be renewed by the teaching of His Word.

Vance began attending our church in 1981. He had been heavily involved in drugs and the occult prior to his first visit to the church. He recently described his experience to me this way:

> My addictions had brought me to a place of hopelessness. I was invited to attend church, and I found Christ. Through the process of listening to the Word of God, personal discipleship, and reading Scripture, my mind was healed and renewed. Today I function as a whole man with positive thinking, and I am living a blessed and empowered life.

4. In God's house, you can find friends, develop a healthy marriage, and raise a family.

God's house plays an important role in people's lives from the day they are born until they depart this earth to be with God in heaven. Babies are dedicated, children are taught the Bible, young people find like-minded friends, couples are married, marriages are strengthened, and parents are encouraged and equipped. Then the cycle repeats. Life is lived generationally, and the church is a central force for good in each generation.

Ryan and Kathy are powerful examples of how God uses the local church to bring healing in the home. They were attending our Red Deer location, but their relationship was not doing well. Ryan was sleeping on the couch, and the marriage was in jeopardy. Then some of our pastors visited their home, and they opened up to them about their struggles.

Ryan said, "Enough is enough. Let's fix this." Since then, their marriage has been totally renewed. Ryan and Kathy are a leading couple in our church today, and their marriage and family are a model for others to follow.

5. In God's house, you can learn a new and better way to live.

There is a right road that leads to life, and there is a wrong road that leads to destruction (Matthew 7:13-14). The world and culture we were born into promote lifestyles, belief systems, and habits that are contrary to the Word of God. Paul wrote to the Ephesian church, "You used to live in sin, just like the rest of the world, obeying the devil . . . All of us used to live that way, following the passionate desires and inclinations of our sinful nature" (Ephesians 2:2).

Church is a place to receive new thoughts, new ways, and new paths. It is part of God's plan to help us navigate the ups and downs and the twists and turns of life. God said through the prophet Isaiah,

> "For my thoughts are not your thoughts,
> neither are your ways my ways,"
> declares the Lord.
> "As the heavens are higher than the earth,
> so are my ways higher than your ways
> and my thoughts than your thoughts."
> (Isaiah 55:8-9)

As we spend time in God's house, our minds are renewed through the Bible, worship, preaching, teaching, counsel, friendship, prayer, and much more. The more time we spend learning about God and enjoying His presence, the more established we become in His way of thinking and living.

The church is a place where people of every culture and experience can come to hear about God. They can bring their friends and family to meet God and learn to walk in His ways and paths, as we read earlier in Isaiah 2.

Frequently God reveals specific paths and decisions to us as we spend time in His presence. Sometimes He will speak to us through worship and prayer, through the message, or through friends at church. Other times He will speak to the church as a whole, whether through prophecy or church leadership, bringing comfort, encouragement, and direction to the congregation. God's house plays a key role in guiding each of us into the plan He has for our lives.

The church is not an add-on experience or a supplement to our already busy lives. It is a central part of God's design for our health and growth. I am thankful for business, government, financial, and educational institutions; but most of all, I am thankful for the church. There is no other organization, community, or assembly that is equal in importance to the house of God. The church is truly the most important place on earth.

THINGS TO THINK ABOUT

1. What are some of God's "ways and paths" you have learned since becoming part of the church?

2. Have you seen God use the church to facilitate healing and health for other people you know? Who do you know who could benefit from becoming planted in God's house and learning His ways?

Daine's Story

When my sister and I were children, my family moved every year. My father's job was to set up gas companies in different cities, so we never stayed long in the same place. At each city or town, my parents would send the two of us to a different church. They never attended themselves, but they made sure we went to the nearest available Alliance, Baptist, or Pentecostal church. I grew up learning about God, but to be honest, I never paid much attention.

Fast forward to 1972. I was twenty-two years old and living in Red Deer. The hippie lifestyle of the sixties and the seventies was normal and natural to my generation, and I had firmly embraced it. I began dating a girl I had liked in high school named Gaylene. Somewhere in between the whirl of alcohol and drugs, she became pregnant. She was living back and forth between Edmonton and Red Deer at the time. Later she told me she had an experience with the Jesus People in Edmonton, but when she moved back to Red Deer, she fell back into her old partying habits. I'm sure I had something to do with that.

The following year I decided to attend college in Calgary. During that time I developed a fascination with Satanism and witchcraft. A friend's girlfriend had dozens of books on the subject, and I couldn't read them fast enough. In retrospect, I was hungry for an authentic spiritual reality. I was searching for God.

Then one day, as I was walking into the living room/kitchen of my basement suite, I suddenly felt God gazing at my heart. I paused in the doorway and looked up. There was nothing visible, yet I saw a beam of light piercing my heart. I knew exactly what it was—or better said, Who it was. I have no idea how long I stood there, stunned and paralyzed, gazing upward. The moment was interrupted when the person I was with asked if I was alright. I mumbled that I was okay; but to myself, I remember saying, "I was looking for God!"

I had no idea what to do next. I called the pastor of the church I had gone to years before and made an appointment to meet with him the next morning. When I arrived the next day, expecting the pastor to lead me to Christ, no one was there. I assumed he forgot, so I got in my car and drove back to Calgary. I found out later the pastor lived on the adjoining property, and he expected me to go there.

When I arrived home, there was a letter waiting for me from my sister, who was living in Edmonton. It was the only letter I've ever received from her, and inside was a tract with a short gospel message and the sinner's prayer. Underneath was a statement: "You cannot put this tract down without making a decision." It was the strangest thing: physically, I couldn't put it down. I dropped to my knees and read the prayer.

I already knew my biggest hindrance to following Jesus would be my friends. It wasn't that they would stop me, but they meant everything to me, and I didn't want to lose them. That day, on my knees in the kitchen, I prayed, "No matter what, even if I lose all my friends, I am turning my life over to Jesus."

I felt that I wasn't going to be able to salvage my school year, even though it was still just a couple months into the fall session, so I decided to go back to Red Deer and figure things out there. In November 1973 I moved home. My parents welcomed me, but I'm not sure what they thought about my conversion. I was very vocal about it—I couldn't stop talking about God and about how instantly He had set me free from drugs and alcohol.

I called a girl I knew from high school named Diane, who had always talked to me about Christ. I used to tease her about it, but I knew she would be interested in knowing I had met Jesus. Diane was involved with a small group of young people who were meeting on Saturday nights with Pastors Mel and Heather Mullen. I remember walking into *that room for the first time and instantly feeling like I was home. There were young people worshiping and singing in the Spirit before the service began, and the presence of God was very tangible.*

Things moved quickly after that. I was water baptized and baptized in the Holy Spirit almost immediately. God sovereignly led me and many others like me to the church because He wanted a generation of hippies and unstructured young people to be discipled. He wanted us to commit our lives to learning and living a daily way of life. This wasn't going to be just church on the weekends. Those days formed the foundation of my life and the lives of many others, and many of those young people became leaders and pillars in the church.

Months passed, and I grew closer to God, but I kept thinking about Gaylene and my new son, Ryan. Diane and Pastor Mel encouraged me to pursue a relationship with them and see where it might go, and I felt it was the right thing to do too. I called Gaylene, and we began meeting for coffee. I shared with her everything that had happened to me.

It turned out God had already prepared her for my dramatic change, because she had experienced the same thing while living in Edmonton. Wisely, she wouldn't have anything to do with me at first, but she did recognize what God had done in my life.

Things progressed rapidly, though. We rekindled our feelings for each other, and on August 30, 1974, we were married. Our wedding was the first one Pastor Mel performed. My son Ryan was seven months old. We were new Christians, newly married, and new parents, and I had started a new career around the same time. The pressures were hard on both of us as we tried to deal with the challenges from each area, but the foundation we were developing in God, along with our church community, added to our commitment to each other, and we made it through.

God has carried us through almost forty-five years of marriage and forty-five years of being planted and fruitful where He has placed us. We are so grateful for His gifts of grace, community, and family!

DAY 31

The Place I *Call* Home
Everyone needs Jesus, and everyone needs a home.

MY SON, JACHIN, often speaks about creating a culture of belonging and acceptance within the church. One day at our staff meeting, he delivered our mission statement: "Everyone Needs Jesus. Everyone Needs a Home." Those words resonated with everyone present. That was exactly what we felt God was asking our church to facilitate. It became clear to us that our church name needed to more accurately reflect who we were becoming.

Our church has changed names several times over the decades. When we began, we were ministering to the needs of youth in Red Deer in the Jesus People era of the 1970s. We named our church People's Church because we wanted to be a church for all people.

During the eighteenth year of our church, we bought a large and very visible property along a main bypass highway. At that time we renamed the church Word of Life. Our mission was to expand into many communities and nations and bring life through the Word of God.

Then we transitioned the church to the next generation of leaders with Jachin as the lead pastor. Soon after that memorable staff meeting, we changed our name to *Home Church*.

The statement Pastor Jachin shared with our staff has had a profound effect on our entire church. *Everyone Needs Jesus. Everyone Needs a Home.* It's more than just a brand or a slogan: it's a belief that has reshaped our culture, attitude, and ministry to people. Home Church is a movement of people who call church *home*. We are a home for people from nations around the world.

YOU BELONG HERE

Home is a place where we belong. It's a place where we are welcome and accepted, a place where we are able to be ourselves.

Matthew Barnett, the pastor of the great Angeles Temple in Los Angeles and the leader of The Dream Center, often says people must know they *belong* before they decide to *believe*. I couldn't agree more.

Christians often get that backward. We think people have to act a certain way before they can be part of our church. That wasn't what Jesus modeled, though. People need to belong, and what better place than the church to provide the safe, warm, inviting environment of HOME?

Pastor Matthew shared a story with me of a man named Brad Alden Mowry. At one time, Brad had all the appearances of success. He was a handsome man in his thirties, a well-known rock musician, the owner of a successful business, married, with two wonderful kids. But his life began to fall apart. He and his wife fought often, and they did not have a Christ-centered marriage. The strife at home led to infidelity, which eventually cost him his family.

He began desperately searching for true meaning in life. One Sunday he wandered into a church. Brad recounts that immediately he felt something different: no one was judging him for his actions, his appearance, or his past. He began attending regularly, and soon he was invited to sing and play on the worship team, even though he still wasn't sure what he believed about God. Then the unexpected began to happen: for the first time in years, he felt like he belonged. Over time, God took hold of his heart and brought him to a place of deep, authentic faith, and it became clear that he was to use his gift of song to glorify God. Eventually, he married a wonderful Christian woman, and his relationship with his two children was restored. Today Brad's music is distributed internationally, and he and his wife Danielle lead worship at churches across the USA and Asia. Recently they even came to Red Deer to lead worship at our church.

Brad's story illustrates the power of belonging. There is something about finding unconditional acceptance that gives people the freedom to ask tough questions, to work through their issues, and to take steps toward recovery. They need a safe environment to heal and grow, and God designed the church to provide just that.

I have always had the practice of shaking hands and sincerely greeting people after the service, especially if they are first-time guests. After I introduce myself to guests, I often say, "I am so glad you came to church today! Welcome, I have just adopted you into our church family." It usually catches them off-guard, and they are pleasantly surprised to be so enthusiastically welcomed to make our church their HOME.

I believe the culture of the church in the twenty-first century will be a *belonging* culture. In more and more churches, there is a sense of family and belonging. When you walk through the doors, you immediately sense, *I belong here. This is my HOME and this is my family.* That is a beautiful gift to people, and it is something our culture desperately needs.

BIRTH AND ADOPTION

People enter the family of God through the process of new birth. Jesus told Nicodemus, "Unless you are born again, you cannot see the Kingdom of God" (John 3:3). This is a spiritual rebirth, of course. Our souls, which were dead because of sin, are made alive through the death and resurrection of Jesus.

Now we are part of the family of God. "To all who believed him and accepted him, he gave the right to become children of God" (John 1:12).

The Bible also uses the metaphor of adoption to illustrate our status as sons and daughters in God's family. God had no obligation to accept us, but in His love and goodness, He has chosen us and made us part of His family. Paul wrote this:

> So you have not received a spirit that makes you fearful slaves. Instead, you received God's Spirit when he adopted you as his own children. Now we call him, "Abba, Father." For his Spirit joins with our spirit to affirm that we are God's children.
> (Romans 8:15-16)

Both metaphors communicate that we are wholly, intentionally, and eternally God's children. We were born into His family through new birth, and we have been adopted as fully privileged children.

Heather and I understand birth and adoption because we have experienced them both—and they are equally beautiful. Our son, Jachin, came into our home through the process of natural birth. Our daughter, Christy, came into our home through the process of adoption. When Jachin was about a year old, a pastor friend from another church in Canada called me and told me an expectant mother had contacted him and said she wanted to give her baby up for adoption at birth. He asked, "Is there someone in your congregation who would be willing to privately adopt a baby?"

I answered, "We will take the baby!" Then I added, "Oh, just a minute. I have to ask my wife first."

I found her and asked, "Heather, would you like to adopt a baby?"

She immediately replied, "Yes! Just get the details."

That phone call set a miracle in motion, and three months later, Christy arrived in our home. Even though she was adopted, she was instantly ours. We often tell people when introducing our children, "Jachin came through natural birth, and Christy came through the telephone. But both are equally loved."

The church is a home for all kinds of people who are brought into the family of God. We must make room for everyone. We must make sure everyone feels equally welcome, regardless of their ethnicity, education, language, economic standing, religious background, family, or failures. God's house is open for all, whether rich or poor; sinners or saints; up-and-coming or down-and-out. Everyone belongs. Everyone has ownership. Everyone has a chair at the table.

WHY HOME?

I could list many benefits and advantages of being in a home, but here are just a few to illustrate my point. As we build churches that people can call HOME, we will see these benefits played out in their lives.

Home is a place to become the person you are meant to be.

Children aren't born fully developed: growth is a long process, and it requires a safe, encouraging, healthy environment. In the same way, new followers of Jesus are not born instantly mature. They need time, love, care, and good examples in order to become the people God designed them to be. God's house is a place where people can grow in maturity, discover and develop their gifts, and learn how to serve. It is a place of spiritual nurturing.

Home is a place to find family.

When my father took his own life, I was left devastated. Over time, God replaced that natural human relationship with spiritual mentors and fathers who came into my life and brought wholeness. God brings healing in place of dysfunction. He takes the separated, the lonely, and the ones who don't belong, and He places them in families. King David wrote, "Father to the fatherless, defender of widows—this is God, whose dwelling is holy. God places the lonely in families" (Psalm 68:5-6).

Home is the very foundation of society. Unfortunately, family values and home stability have eroded greatly in culture today. That makes the church even more necessary, because for many, it offers the family and friendship they have not found elsewhere. God's house is not designed to replace family relationships, but it does help fill in the gaps if families have fallen apart. And as people learn how to have healthy relationships within the church, they often begin to see changes in their natural family relationships as well.

Home is a place of covering and protection.

Home is meant to be a safe place. It is a shelter, a refuge, and a defense against the hostility and danger in the world. The church provides spiritual safety and protection for people. Instead of facing the world alone, they can surround themselves with people who care for them and watch out for them. If people are sick, they can find healing. If they are hungry, they can find sustenance. If they are lonely, they can find authentic love. If they are fearful, they can find peace. If they are weak, they can find strength.

I could go on for many pages more, because I believe with all my heart that the church is a God-given blessing that is just as relevant today as it was in Bible times. This isn't just theological speculation—I have seen the church bring the healing, hope, and life of Jesus to person after person, family after family, community after community, and even nation after nation. For decades now I've marveled at the power of God at work in His people. I have seen it, lived it, and loved every minute of it. God's church is not an afterthought or a parenthesis or a footnote in His plan. It is His thoughtfully designed, generous gift to humanity.

As I conclude, I say to you, *Welcome Home!* You are always welcome with Jesus, and you are always welcome in His church.

THINGS TO THINK ABOUT:

1. What does the word "home" mean to you?

2. Why do people need a place to belong?

3. How can you help make your church a home for people?

THANK YOU for your love for Jesus and your commitment to His church! I am grateful for the opportunity to have shared with you some of the things I've learned during my walk with Jesus. Life is truly a gift, and the more we experience Jesus and His church, the greater and more abundant that life becomes.

I want to leave you with a call to action: to put into practice what you have read in these pages. I trust this book has been a blessing and a challenge to you, no matter where you are in your walk with Jesus. If you have not yet made a decision to follow Him, then I pray that through this book, you would have a greater understanding of who He is: His love for you, His commitment to you, and His reality in your life. If you have been a follower of Jesus for some time, then I pray this book would encourage you to not only love Jesus more, but to have a greater understanding of the church and a greater commitment to building it.

Jesus is building His church, the greatest entity on earth. Every community needs a vibrant local church that can bring life and hope to everyone nearby, a church that is committed to reaching people with the love of Jesus.

Will you make a commitment today to love Jesus like never before and to step into your God-given calling to help build His church?

SPECIAL THANKS

I WISH TO thank Pastor Brian Houston and the Hillsong Network who have played a major role in the changes we made in our church. For many years I have traveled to Sydney to attend the Hillsong Conference, ask questions, receive input, and bring home ideas to help our church.

I am grateful that in recent years, Home Church has been strongly influenced by the ministry of Kevin Gerald and the team of leaders from Champion Centre as well as the Team Church conferences.

I also wish to thank Tommy and Matthew Barnett for their great friendship and relationship of encouragement along the journey.

With the influence of these great leaders, as well as my personal pastor, Mel Davis, *Experience Jesus and His Church* is a book to advance God's great church in the world.

Mel C. Mullen